insight text guide

Diana Barnes

False Claims of Colonial Thieves

Charmaine Papertalk Green and John Kinsella

First published in 2022, reprinted in 2024.

Insight Publications Pty Ltd
3/350 Charman Road
Cheltenham VIC 3192
Australia
Tel: +61 3 8571 4950
Email: books@insightpublications.com.au

www.insightpublications.com.au

A catalogue record for this book is available from the National Library of Australia

Charmaine Papertalk Green and John Kinsella's False Claims of Colonial Thieves / Diana Barnes

Diana Barnes asserts the moral right to be identified as the author of this work.

ISBNs:
9781922378132 (print)
9781922378149 (digital)

Cover design by Gisela Beer

Proudly Printed in Australia by Ligare Book Printers

contents

Theme summary table iv

Overview 1

About the authors 1

Background & context 3

Genre, structure & language 5

Poem-by-poem analysis 10

Themes, ideas & values 60

Different interpretations 68

Questions & answers 71

Sample answer 78

References & reading 81

THEME SUMMARY TABLE

Theme	Poets' attitude	Poems
Yarning	Respectful approach to learning about First Nations culture via dialogue and the exchange of stories	'Simply Yarning'; 'Yarn Response Poem'; 'Hawes – God's Intruder'; 'Campfire'; 'Tangi'; 'Epilogue'
Decolonisation	Commitment to undercutting residual colonial ideas and attitudes	'Hawes – God's Intruder'; 'Honey to Lips Bottlebrush'; 'Lake Magic Resonances (January 2017)'; 'Funeral Directors'; 'The Wild Colonial Boy'
Barna	Wajarri word for country or earth, reflecting the importance of belonging and having a strong relationship to the land	'Undermining'; 'Fe Fi Fo Fum'; 'Don't mine me'; 'Hawes – God's Intruder'; 'I won't pretend'; 'Campfire'; 'Tangi'; 'Strong Wajarri Man'; 'Epilogue'
Environment-alism	Condemnation of farming and mining activities, and government policy, which cause devastating environmental degradation	'Sammies (Salmon Gums)'; 'Blue Scar'; 'The Great Western Woodlands'; 'Blue Hazmat Suits in the Coolbellup Bush Prior to its Destruction'; 'Cathedral Avenue'
Religion/ Christianity	View that western religion is part of the colonial machine that displaces First Nations communities and histories	'Undermining'; 'Hawes – God's Intruder'; 'The Artlessness of Internal Travel'; 'Bottlebrush Behind Our Lady of Fatima Church, Nanson, Chapman Valley'; 'Honey to Lips Bottlebrush'; 'Our Lady of Mt Carmel, Mullewa'; 'No other road'; 'I don't like flying over'; 'On Julie Dowling's *My White Friend*, Geraldton Regional Gallery, 2017'
Family	Belief that family is a source of personal identity to be actively nurtured, and a source of values to be carefully scrutinised	'Grandmothers'; 'Funeral Directors'; 'Hawes – God's Intruder'; 'No other road'; 'Respect'; 'Niagara Dam Poems'; 'Histories'; 'Tangi'; 'Nganayungu Yagu'; 'A White Colonial Boy'; 'The Salt Chronicles'; 'Our Lady of Mt Carmel, Mullewa'; 'The Artlessness of Internal Travel'; 'Yarn Response Poem'; 'Blue Hazmat Suits in the Coolbellup Bush Prior to its Destruction'; 'Drug Slaves'

OVERVIEW

False Claims of Colonial Thieves (2018) is a poetry collection written by two contemporary Australian poets, Charmaine Papertalk Green and John Kinsella. Both writers are well established, with a number of prior publications. Both are from Western Australia: Green is a First Nations woman; Kinsella is a male descendant of white settlers. The collection brings together two contrasting voices to form a dialogue about the legacy of colonialism in Australia today.

This legacy is the primary focus of *False Claims of Colonial Thieves,* and characters and relationships are considered through that lens. Although the poems present a number of characters and relationships, they are not detailed portraits. Several character impressions can be pieced together from passing comments made across the collection and from this we can also infer relationships. Some of the poems are dedicated to friends and associates of the poets, and this is another way that the social world of the poetry is defined.

When analysing poetry, it is important to keep in mind that, when a poet writes in a personal voice (with statements beginning with 'I'), this might be the speech or thought of a fictional persona rather than a direct opinion of the individual poet. Nonetheless this collection of poetry does use autobiographical details that match what is known of the poets' lives, and therefore it is reasonable to assume in most cases that the 'I' does refer to the poets themselves, or at least a version of themselves that they have crafted to present to their readers.

About the authors

Charmaine Papertalk Green is a Yamaji poet. Her mother is of the Wajarri and Amangu people and her father of the Badimaya people of Western Australia. She was born in 1962 at Eradu railway siding between Mullewa and Geraldton in Western Australia. She grew up in

Mullewa and now lives and works in Geraldton. Green has published many volumes of poetry, and has won various Australian literary awards, including the 2020 Victorian Premier's Prize for Poetry, and the 2020 Australian Literary Society Gold Medal for *Nganajungu Yagu* (2019), a collection of poems and letters on the theme of mothers. Her poetry appears in important anthologies of Australian poetry including *The Penguin Book of Australian Women Poets* (1986) and *Inside Black Australia: An Anthology of Aboriginal Poetry* (1988). Green is also a practising visual artist and an academic in the field of Aboriginal health.

John Kinsella was born in Perth in 1963. His mother was a poet and he has been writing poetry all his life. He grew up moving between Perth, the country around Mullewa, and Geraldton. He has published more than thirty volumes of poetry, drama and nonfiction, and has won various literary awards, including the Western Australian Premier's Book Award three times. His poetry is widely anthologised. Like Green, Kinsella is also an academic. He is a fellow at Churchill College (University of Cambridge), an Emeritus Professor at Curtin University, Western Australia, and he has taught in the United States. Kinsella has edited poetry anthologies, founded the literary magazine *Salt*, and is an international editor for *The Kenyon Review*. Unlike many contemporary poets, Kinsella has a long history of creative collaboration, including with Western Australian writer Dorothy Hewett.

The Green–Kinsella collaboration began in 2004 when the pair met in Western Australia. Since that time, they have been 'yarning' or exchanging stories. They share ideas, develop their thoughts, and co-write poems via email. What they have in common is a political outlook on Australian culture and society. In a joint 2018 interview on the ABC's *The Book Show* Green admitted that she is not in dialogue with many white men, descendants of colonial settlers, but that this friendship and collaboration is possible because Kinsella really understands what the arrival of white settlers meant for her people (Nichols 2018). Kinsella holds the radical view that all Australian land should be returned to its original First Nations owners.

BACKGROUND & CONTEXT

Authors' historical context

Green and Kinsella grew up in the 1960s and 70s, a time when the colonial ethos of white Australia dominated the cultural landscape. The settler–colonial attitude was that Australian land belonged to no one (was considered terra nullius) prior to the arrival of Europeans, and that it was a resource to be farmed and mined for profit. In 1964 prominent journalist, academic and social critic Donald Horne declared Australia 'the lucky country'. This phrase gained currency because it seemed to describe accurately the high standard of living enjoyed by white Australians at the time. Later Horne explained that he did not have this in mind; rather, he was referring to 'the idea of Australia ... whose prosperity in the great age of manufacturing came from the luck of its historical origins ... we have never "earned" our democracy. We simply went along with some British habits' (1976). During the 1970s it became increasingly clear that the veneer of British attitudes that had defined the Australian ethos was coming unstuck. In 1972 Gough Whitlam was elected Prime Minister: the campaign slogan 'It's time' succinctly expressed the party's core promise to break Australia's colonial ties to Britain.

While Green and Kinsella were growing up, mining became an increasingly divisive political issue. The worldwide nuclear disarmament movement fuelled a public outcry over French nuclear testing in the Pacific between 1972 and 1973; this was followed by the 1976–77 debate about uranium mining in Australia. Things shifted dramatically in 1992 with a landmark case in the High Court of Australia. The 'Mabo decision' overturned the concept of terra nullius and recognised the land rights of the Meriam people, traditional owners of Mer (Murray Islands) in the Torres Strait, fuelling a process of reckoning that was partly legal (resulting in the Commonwealth *Native Title Act 1993*) and partly cultural.

Mullewa is a small inland town, with a population of just over 400 people, in the wheatbelt region north of Perth. It is situated in country belonging to the Wajarri people. When European settlers moved into the area to establish farms, from 1869, conflict with the Wajarri ensued. Lives were lost on both sides, and in her poetry Green expresses bitterness over this history and writes about sites that had significance for her people. During the 1890s, Mullewa was an important stopover between Geraldton and the goldfields in Murchison. Today, tourists visit to see the spectacular show of wildflowers in the spring. The area is also known for Yamaji Art, a gallery and studio that is owned and operated by Aboriginal artists.

Geraldton is also referred to frequently in *False Claims of Colonial Thieves*. Lying on the coast 100 kilometres from Mullewa, it has a population of more than 37 000 people. It is situated on the traditional land of the Amangu people, with Nanda and Badimaya peoples nearby. Today, First Nations peoples of the Geraldton–Mullewa region usually identify as Yamaji (as Green does) or Wajarri. Contact with Europeans has a particularly long history in this region, dating back to the arrival of Dutch explorers in the 1500s and 1600s. The township was established in the early 1850s after the discovery of iron ore in the area.

Publishing context and history

False Claims of Colonial Thieves is published by Magabala Books, an Aboriginal-owned not-for-profit publishing house based in Broome, Western Australia. It is supported by government and philanthropic funding. Magabala is dedicated to publishing Indigenous Australian writing across a range of genres. It was established in 1984 with the express purpose of preserving Aboriginal and Torres Strait Islander stories, and supporting emerging writers.

False Claims of Colonial Thieves is an unusual publishing venture. Rarely is poetry published in a dialogical format that underlines the collaborative nature of its composition.

GENRE, STRUCTURE & LANGUAGE

Genre

False Claims of Colonial Thieves is a collection of poems concerned with identity and specific locations. The technical term for this is topographical poetry, meaning poetry of place. As the earliest theorists of this genre realised, topographical poetry never simply documents a region: it always probes a little deeper to consider the meaning of the town, building, church, land, park or river concerned; the values it represents; and the kind of society it supports. Often, topographical poetry documents reality in order to guide readers to see that better alternatives are possible. As Wiradjuri poet Jeanine Leane (2020) wrote in her review of *False Claims of Colonial Thieves*: 'Poetry can do what history cannot. This book begins the difficult, long overdue yet essential-for-the-future-of-race-relations – and healing – that Australia needs to have about place, belonging, her/histories and truth telling'.

In *False Claims of Colonial Thieves* Green and Kinsella probe how places and their histories reflect Australian social values. They trace an ongoing conflict over those values, asking readers to examine underlying attitudes. Their poetry participates in the topographical poetic tradition of imagining ideal worlds and teaching readers to believe in them. In this volume Green and Kinsella focus particularly on the small town of Mullewa and the surrounding region of Geraldton in Western Australia. This involves telling stories about the history of particular places: for example, the arrival of settler–colonials in Australia; the appropriation of First Nations land; the establishment of farms and a pastoral economy; and the building of mines; but also the histories of First Nations peoples. Green and Kinsella tell this story together, from two sides of the fence, so to speak: one the descendent of the First Nations peoples displaced by European settlement, the other the descendant of white people who farmed and managed mines in the district. Kinsella never speaks for

Green, nor does Green speak for Kinsella. Green describes First Nations peoples' relation to certain places and her own familial connection and experience, and Kinsella recounts the white settler perspective and his own history as a descendant of farmers, mining engineers and managers. By braiding their voices together, the poets demonstrate that the way forward is respectful dialogue. The poets speak their individual truths, describe their origins and map their future; nobody is silenced or dominant. The ideal they imagine is embodied in their dialogue: together the poets experiment in a new multi-voiced way of accounting for the past and developing ideals for the future.

Structure

Within the collection the poetry takes a number of different forms: some poems are arranged in verse, some in numbered sections, some in dialogue. The poems vary in length. None follows a strict rhyme scheme. In most, the poets address the reader, a third party or each other directly, as though speaking from their own experience.

The structure of the volume as a whole is dialogical (involving a conversation) and multi-voiced (containing multiple voices). It is unusual for contemporary poets to compose and publish together. Clearly the volume was born of collaboration, but Kinsella and Green's individual authorship remains clear. Most of the poems in the collection are single-authored, and the final line of each of these is followed by 'JK' or 'CPG' to designate authorship. Several poems are co-written; in these (apart from 'Epilogue'), alternating segments are attributed to each poet, giving the impression that the poems document a conversation. This effect of a dialogue between the poets is maintained throughout the collection; many of the single-authored poems are in pairs or groups of poems on a similar theme. For example, the co-written poem 'Hawes – God's Intruder', about the Roman Catholic priest Monsignor John Hawes and the church he designed and built in Mullewa, is followed by Kinsella's 'Bottlebrush Behind Our Lady of Fatima Church, Nanson, Chapman

Valley', Green's 'Honey to Lips Bottlebrush', then Kinsella's 'Our Lady of Mt Carmel, Mullewa'. These poems work together as a group; it is as though the dialogue established in 'Hawes – God's Intruder' is continued in the three single-authored poems that follow. Each poem is distinct, as is each poet's voice, and yet they demand to be read together as ruminations on a common theme from a range of perspectives.

Language

Traditionally poetic language differs from spoken language, dramatic language and the language of prose. Poetic language is more likely to employ rhetorical devices such as alliteration, metaphor, hyperbole, repetition and simile. For example, *'Dig it up / Blow it up / Crush it up / Poison it up / Ship it out'* (Green, 'Selfish warriors', p.10, ll.12–16) uses rhythmic repetition with minor variations to emphasise the relentlessly exploitative logic of mining, while the couplet 'Hills broken into millions of pieces / Deep cuts into the flesh of earth' (Green, 'Dream mine time animals', p.8, ll.11–12) uses a simile likening the land to a living human or animal body.

Visual distortion is another poetic technique employed; for example, consider the following lines from Green's poem 'Don't mine me' (p.14):

King

    Queen

        Government

            Economy

                Asia

                    PROFIT (ll.9–14).

The visual presentation of these lines on the page makes them stand out from the rest of the poem. First, they are in italics, whereas the rest of the poem is not. Second, they are arranged in a sequence of increasing indents to give the impression of a staircase of words; by contrast, the rest of the poem is aligned to the left margin. Such visual elements guide the reader to pay particular attention to certain words and lines.

Intertextual references (allusions to other literary or non-literary texts) are also used; for example, Green's line '*Gimme money money money*' quotes the ABBA song 'Money, Money, Money' (1976), to emphasise the greed of Traditional Owners who sell out their own culture ('Selfish warriors', p.10, l.18).

Ekphrasis (description of a visual art work within literature) provides an opportunity to reflect upon the nature and function of art, as in Kinsella's 'On Julie Dowling's *My White Friend*, Geraldton Regional Gallery, 2017' (p.105) and Green's 'Old Girl' (p.94).

Green and Kinsella write in **the vernacular** (everyday local language). Green captures the turn of phrase and words of First Nations speakers, and Kinsella replicates the language of his contemporaries and family. This language is idiomatic (natural to the speakers). Making poetry from Australian spoken language has a political point. It is a way of insisting that Australian culture is not defined by 'proper' English, the language of the colonisers. Both Green and Kinsella have reason to distance themselves from Englishness. As Kinsella says, the English language represents 'the chains and slavery of the languages / of occupation' ('The Wild Colonial Boy', p.135, ll.14–15). By writing poetry in the Australian vernacular, Kinsella and Green express what the Australian poet Les Murray called 'the vernacular republic' (1982), that is, a strong vision of Australia as culturally and politically independent of Great Britain.

One quality that makes Green and Kinsella's vernacular language poetic is their use of code switching and juxtaposition (contrast) to jump from one kind of language, tone or allusion to another. This is achieved through:

- linguistic shifts: for example, Green splices Wajarri words and phrases into her poems, as in the line 'Finding time to walk over / Each other's barna' ('I won't pretend', p.62, ll.16–17)

- blends of discourses: for example, Kinsella draws scientific terms and concepts into his poems about mining, as in 'mobs / of sheep don't "split like mercury"' ('Red Lead, Almost Dead', p.25, ll.9–10), where a scientific concept provides a simile
- homonyms (words with multiple meanings): for example, the title of the first poem in the volume, Kinsella's 'Undermining' (p.1) refers to both a tendency to belittle others, and to excavation for mining. The word suggests a connection between the two activities. In 'Prologue' Kinsella writes: 'And so the mining companies reach into our schools, / funding programs that make students in their own image, / filling the holes they make in country with propaganda' ('Prologue', p.xi, ll.4–6). Kinsella shifts from the idea of holes dug into the earth by mining companies to the idea of holes as conceptual gaps in values and ideas.

The words of songs are called 'lyrics' because they exhibit the personal heart-to-heart quality of lyrical poetry. Green and Kinsella's poems are frequently **lyrical** (written in a personal voice). This creates the impression that the speaker/voice (persona) in the poem has an intimate rapport with the reader.

At times *False Claims of Colonial Thieves* is **didactic**; that is, it tells readers directly what to believe. It insists that readers should distrust the lies that serve beneficiaries of the colonial system that continues to dominate the government and economy of Australia. Didacticism is reinforced through imperatives (authoritative commands) such as, 'Don't crawl into a / Dark corner of cultural nothingness' (Green, 'Yamaji Culture', p.66, ll.16–17).

POEM-BY-POEM ANALYSIS

Prologue, JK, and Prologue Response, CPG (p.xi)

In the seven-line opening poem, 'Prologue', Kinsella reveals his political agenda: to oppose the mining industry and its insidious thought control. His critique is directed squarely at the values embedded in young Australians via education. He calls it 'propaganda / sold as learning' (ll.5–6), a story promoted for political ends, particularly by governments.

In 'Prologue Response', a six-line poetic reply, Green affirms the activist agenda Kinsella establishes. She declares that 'the / privileged are privilege blind' (ll.5–6), and the authorities, including 'environmental scientists' (l.2), veil 'what lies on or within country' (l.4).

Key point

In this pair of poems, the poets assert a hopeful vision of what poetry can achieve: it can speak truth to power; it can raise awareness in readers; and it can challenge dominant taken-for-granted ideologies (systems of ideas and values that underpin political, economic and social outlooks).

Key vocabulary

Stygofauna: creatures, or fauna, that live in water underground.

Q How do these introductory poems prepare the reader for what follows?

Undermining, JK & CPG (pp.1–2)

This poem is made up of two numbered parts: the first by Kinsella and the second by Green. The poem concerns mining: in particular, the proposed open-cut uranium mine at Wiluna. Uranium mining has faced considerable opposition in Australia, and a six-year ban ended in 2008. The Japanese Fukushima nuclear reactor disaster of 2011 only intensified the protests. Since 2016, the mining company Toro has held rights to mine uranium at Wiluna, but uranium prices must rise to make developing the site economically viable. This poem enters these debates and, as its title forewarns, asserts that by digging deep under the earth's surface, mining degrades the environment and compromises human values.

Part 1, by Kinsella, comprises seven discrete sentences with a line of space between each. It opens:

> The king brown does not die from its own poison – within its body, inert.
>
> Uranium within the hold of old ground around Wiluna is more than history. Leave it there. Intact. (part 1, ll.1–4)

Here Kinsella makes an analogy between the king brown snake and the uranium at Wiluna. Both are potentially lethal, but neither will harm us if left undisturbed. In the words 'Scrub, forests, / their contents. All gone. Hole' (part 1, ll.9–10), Kinsella mourns the inevitable destruction of the natural environment that mining will cause.

Part 2, Green's contribution, comprises twenty-seven short lines presented as one continuous stanza. It opens with the couplet: 'Balu winja barna real winja / Real old ones them ones' (part 2, ll.15–16). The mix of English with Wajarri, the language of the Wajarri people of the Wiluna region, signals that part 2 is written from a very different perspective. With the aid of the Glossary (pp.146–7), we can translate the Wajarri roughly as 'Him old country, real old'. This opening line, then, makes another kind of political claim: this is unceded Wajarri land. The mining venture Kinsella describes violates western ethical standards, fuels war, *and* destroys First Nations history, tradition and cultural heritage. The Wajarri words remind English-speaking readers that they cannot fully comprehend this loss. This couplet is repeated in the middle and in closing: its implications dominate part 2.

Key point

Kinsella and Green present a sympathetic dialogue on the impacts of mining but their voices remain differentiated. Parts 1 and 2 of 'Undermining' are characterised by the distinct insights, linguistic range and cultural perspective of each poet, but united by their shared political protest over mining in Western Australia.

Q How is dialogue established in 'Undermining'?

Grandmothers, JK & CPG (pp.3–6)

'Grandmothers' is a dialogue poem made up of four unnumbered parts: the first and third by Kinsella, and the second and fourth by Green.

Part 1

Kinsella describes his paternal grandmother, a mining-town child whose 'father was foreman / of the South Champion mine' (ll.2–3), and whose son, Kinsella's father, worked in mines at 'Karratha and Kal' or Kalgoorlie (l.4). The grandmothers theme leads Kinsella to reflect on his position as the offspring of a mining family. This familial history gives him licence to declare 'so it's not as if I come to the mines / without foreknowledge' (ll.5–6).

Rather than present this legacy as a burden of guilt, Kinsella draws upon his insider knowledge – of the operation of mines, their commercial imperatives and the associated personal costs – to strengthen his assertion that mines do not operate 'for the sake of community, / but ... to fuel the world's end' (ll.12–13, 14).

Part 2

Following an asterisk dividing the sections, Green opens: 'My grandmother washed / White town fella's clothes / To feed her kids and survive' (ll.15–17). This portrait directly builds on Kinsella's by telling the story of a woman who served white households like that of Kinsella's grandmother. For Green's grandmother, survival was the primary focus.

As she died before large-scale mining was established, it was Green who, as a child, watched 'rail wagons' (l.26) of Koolanooka iron ore 'Rolling' (l.27) through the town, without comprehending 'what this meant / Or where this country was going' (ll.29–30). Like Kinsella, Green considers her familial relationship to mining and its impact on Western Australian regional communities.

Green uses expressions such as 'White town fella's clothes' (l.16) and 'Out pass Morawa way' (l.25), to capture her grandmother's language. This Aboriginal–English dialect, sometimes called 'pidgin English', is simplified language used for communication between groups who have different first languages. Pidgin speakers may have mistaken 'pass' for 'past' or 'fella' for 'fellow' because they had not seen the words written, but now Green uses these misspoken words with pride. Green's grandmother was disadvantaged by being forced to speak in the coloniser's tongue. Green captures her grandmother's uncertain and stumbling grasp of her oppressors' alien language, and yet also stands outside that language practice to comment on it. The closing line 'I was just a kid watching trains' (l.32) implies that now she is a mature adult and practising poet with a well-honed ability to manipulate both the English tongue and First Nations languages at will.

Part 3

In the third section of 'Grandmothers', Kinsella reflects on his grandmother's stories of his great-grandfather 'lost in the desert being saved / by an Elder and Afghan cameleer' (ll.37–8), and of how 'she "watched the blackfellas" / through the hessian curtains' (ll.68–9). These stories stimulate his own imaginative response to the past. For example, of his great-grandfather's desert rescue he writes, 'As a child, I was obsessed with this / story and it made the dry spaces / lush and hopeful' (ll.39–41). He thinks about what his ancestor may have learned through this experience, reflecting, 'In my great- / grandfather's delirium, he heard / the many voices of the desert' (ll.41–3) and 'He knew the language / he couldn't understand was so complex / it was drawn out of the rock, the plants, / the very essence of the ground he was / robbing' (ll.49–53).

This is a reconstruction of the past. Kinsella admits that he cannot know what his ancestors thought; he asserts, 'My grandmother told me many stories / of the desert. Of flowers and birds / on the edges. I am free to retell her stories' (ll.63–5). Thus Kinsella presents his grandmother as the source of family stories, told from the sidelines of the mining activities that occupied the men in his family. Recognising his grandmother as an innocent observer, he yearns: 'if only / she understood how to see' (ll.74–5). Nevertheless, she left her poet grandson rich memories to retell and embroider at will.

Part 4

Green's closing contribution to 'Grandmothers' opens, 'There were no nanna Alice stories' (l.76), highlighting a gap in the record: some people disappear from family histories. Green speculates that her mother did not mention nanna Alice as the memory was too painful. She finds evidence of her short life in 'the Native Welfare files' (l.82), the documentary records of the Western Australian Government's Native Welfare Office (1955–72) which regulated the 'care' of Aboriginal children not already wards of the state under the *Child Welfare Act 1947*. Green cannot reminisce over her nanna's stories – this luxury is not available – but she can sit by her grave in Geraldton, 'Whispering secrets to a nanna / Telling her stories of country / Her descendants and their lives' (ll.86–8). Her only satisfaction is that nanna predeceased the mining boom.

Q What family histories do Kinsella and Green associate with their grandmothers?

Key vocabulary

Kookynie: mining town in the Eastern Goldfields of Western Australia, now a ghost town.

Karratha: mining town in the Pilbara region of Western Australia; centre of iron ore mining, managed by Hamersley Iron.

Western Mining: originally established as a Kalgoorlie goldmining company in 1933, taken over by BHP Billiton in 2005.

Morawa: town north of Perth in Western Australia's wheatbelt region.

Koolanooka iron ore: from the Koolanooka iron ore mine, twenty kilometres east of Morawa.

Tailings: waste materials from ore extraction.

Afghan cameleers / 'Ghans': camel drivers in outback Australia in the 1860s to 1930s.

Miner's disease: lung disease, pneumoconiosis, caused by regular exposure to airborne dust particles.

Don't want me to talk, CPG (p.7)

Green addresses this twenty-eight-line poem to an undefined 'you' who does not want her 'to talk about / Mining or its impact on Country' (ll.1–2), 'The concept and construct of "whiteness"' (l.4), or any other element of the impact of the settler–colonial legacy on First Nations peoples in present-day Australia. This makes the reader uncomfortable, as the persona addressed as 'you' is not sympathetic. It becomes clear that 'you' is a generalised reference to bigoted white Australia in general. Worst of all: 'You don't want me to talk about / How I have got a voice / And you don't listen' (ll.26–8).

The poem records the bias of white consciousness, narratives and histories, and creates a counter-narrative (a story that unsettles the dominant account). The repeated negative title phrase asserts that, contrary to what 'you want', this Yamaji poet has a voice, and she challenges the once-standard white history of Australia's settlement. Green narrates a counter-history of 'Invasion' (l.11), 'Past injustices, cultural cruelty, cultural genocide / And the cultural pain that is left behind' (ll.14–15).

Key point

Although 'reconciliation' is 'the wrong word / On its own and without truth' (ll.18–19), and it will take more than a word to heal, the repeated line 'It's a shared true history – let's heal' (ll.12, 16) injects the poem with a note of hope about the future.

Q What pathway towards healing does Green propose?

Dream mine time animals, CPG (p.8)

Green imagines the mined landscape as a nightmare Dreamtime that future generations will inherit. The children of tomorrow will 'proudly tell / Their stories around campfires / Of the mechanical snakes slithering across land' (ll.3–5). Rather than following the First Nations tradition of attributing sentience (feeling) to country and anthropomorphising (humanising) animals, Green imagines her descendants viewing mining machinery as sentient. It is true that people tend to look back on their past with nostalgia, and warp their recollection of the past to fit their current purposes, but here it is exaggerated to the point of absurdity to highlight the cultural vacuum left in the wake of mining. The second stanza brings this negative legacy into view with its descriptions of the 'Gaping wounds' (l.13) on the body of the land. Green speculates that future generations will consider the 'Man-made hills' (l.17) of slag heaps as part of their 'country, tradition and culture' (l.18), and 'weave [them] into song lines' (l.19).

Q How does the idea of sentience give emotional depth to this poem?

Key vocabulary

Haulpak: brand of off-road mining truck, in use from 1953 to around 1999.

Country rulers, CPG (p.9)

This is an angry poem that demands that readers acknowledge Australia's brutal history. In settling 'this country of milk and money / And iron ore, iron ore' (ll.1–2), white colonists exploited the goodwill of First Nations peoples, who 'showed' the land to the 'Grandparents or parents' of current white rulers, and then those settlers 'stole it' from them (ll.22, 23, 27). The opening line misquotes the biblical 'land of milk and honey', the promised land of the Jews (described in the Old Testament book of Exodus), replacing it with 'milk and money'. Green identifies greed as the root cause of the exploitation and violation, and suggests this attitude is propped up by Christianity.

Q What is the implied answer to the question 'Who are the real rulers of the country?' (l.4)?

Selfish warriors, CPG (pp.10–11)

Green criticises First Nations 'warriors' who claim land rights over country appropriated by settler–colonials, only to sell those rights back to mining companies and thus enable the destruction of First Nations lands to serve white capitalism.

Q What most angers Green?

Fe Fi Fo Fum, CPG (p.12)

Here Green adapts the giant's refrain 'Fe Fi Fo Fum' from the 'Jack and the Beanstalk' fairy story to represent the logic that fuels the mining industry; for example, 'Fe Fi Fo Fum / Decked out in flouros *[sic]* / Here they come / I smell a mining robot chum' (ll.18–21). The poem uses the naive language and rhyme schemes of playground chants to describe mining activities: 'Airport stampede of / Yellow, silver, orange, gold / Time with family, community, / Children now sold sold sold' (ll.6–9).

The rhythms of children's language emphasise certain bald facts: the amorality of mining and the moribund (almost dead) cultural landscape left in its wake.

In 'Jack and the Beanstalk', Jack and his mother are poor. To get some money, she sends him to sell their cow, but he trades it for magic beans. Jack's mother throws the beans out of the window in anger. By morning a giant beanstalk has grown; Jack climbs up and finds a giant's castle. The giant chants threateningly: 'Fe Fi Fo Fum / I smell the blood of an Englishman / Be he alive or be he dead / I'll grind his bones to make my bread' ('Jack and the Giant Killer', 1711).

In the folk tale, Jack and his mother get the better of the giant, stealing from and killing him. By contrast, in Green's poem the chant threatens miners and those who profit from mining, and exploit the land for 'bread'. If we follow the analogy to its logical end, then, Green seems to warn that an unlikely hero like Jack will topple the mining industry, but this new Jack will be motivated by personal gain, and the circuit of greed will be displaced but not broken.

Q How does Green use the language of folk tales to critique mining?

Fluoro girl world, CPG (p.13)

The opening lines of this poem reference Madonna's 1985 song 'Material Girl' and/or Aqua's 1997 song 'Barbie Girl', which might at first seem frivolous, until it becomes apparent that Green is referring to miners' fluorescent safety gear. See more discussion in the 'Themes, ideas & values' section (pp.60–7).

Don't mine me, CPG (p.14)

This protest poem is built around the colloquial polite phrase 'don't mind me'. Green replaces 'mind' with 'mine' and repeats the phrase mockingly. The replacement does not entirely overwrite the meaning of 'mine', rather, each time one of these words is used it also registers the other. For example, in the lines, 'I think all the time about minding / This land for the next generations' (ll.4–5), 'mind' is readily replaced by 'mine' – substituting exploitation and selfishness for intergenerational care. The closing line reads, 'Don't mind me and don't mine me' (l.23). Strangely, this insistent and repeated request to ignore the speaker works to draw attention rather than divert it.

Q What does Green want her reader to mind?

Niagara Dam Poems: Eastern Goldfields, Western Australia (Wongai Country), JK (pp.15–17)

This four-part poem is a meditation on the Niagara Dam, built near Kalgoorlie, Western Australia, in the late 1800s to provide water for steam trains.

1 Floodways in desert

The opening stanza introduces the flood plains at the edge of the desert, the poet's familial connection to that landscape, and a foreboding classical allusion to Roman history (see 'Themes, ideas and values', pp.60–7). When Kinsella writes of dry riverbeds 'where my grandmother / played as a child' (ll.2–3), he establishes the locus (place) of this poem, and identifies his own connection to it through his grandmother's innocent play. The mines are 'so deep' that 'they drowned' (ll.12–13). The tone is sombre and ominous but it is not clear who has drowned: perhaps the once-dry riverbanks, which were flooded to make way for the dam; or symbolically, innocence has died, suggested by the image of the child who once played in a landscape that is now toxic and inhospitable as a result of mining.

2 Revamped

Here Kinsella describes rewilding (re-establishing natural processes) at the site of the human-made dam. He notes that 'green water' (l.19) ebbs against the 'grey skin' (l.14), or concrete, of the dam wall; he sees birdlife in the 'fairy-martins hangnest' (l.22) and insects or 'midgies ... swarm' (l.24–5); 'roo scats' (l.25) suggest that kangaroos drink there. The encroachment of animals and insects on the built environment 'has revamped / pioneer myths' (ll.28–9). The pioneer myth of mastering the wild landscape and channelling its resources towards human progress falls apart when nature resumes control.

3 On the desert shores

This stanza continues the theme of the anomaly of a desert waterhole. Descriptions of the weather, landscape and wildlife convey the ominous sense that the unsettling of the natural order brought on by this dam may be a forewarning of ill to come. As clouds close in and 'a rare front darkens over' (l.35), the desert plants are 'troubled / at gatherings of water' (ll.39–40). The small Australian native waterbird, the 'young grebe' (l.43) is 'glancing at array / of rock as another's geology' (ll.46–7). These rocks, 'rose quartz / apricot quartz / scattered finds' (ll.32–4), do not belong here; they were brought to the surface when Niagara Dam was created.

4 Night parrots affront

In the final stanza the darkening weather front brings 'wind driving hard' (l.49); the 'heavens can-opener camper vans ... pipping them at posts' (ll.54–6). The holiday-makers on '*Around Australia*' (l.55) tours are defeated by the weather. But 'the night parrot / affronting accomplices / here in force / in the middle / of a rare dark day / though lightning against the glare' (ll.60–5) suggests some hope for renewal. The night parrot is an elusive bird, listed as Critically Endangered under WA's Biodiversity Conservation Act. It was thought to have been extinct since 1912, until scientists discovered some in Queensland in 2013 and a population was photographed in Western Australia in 2017. Kinsella's night parrots appear 'in force'; they alone are impervious to the unseasonable weather that ruffles the zebra finches and defeats the tourists.

Key vocabulary

Wongai Country: goldfields region between Esperance and Nullarbor.

Sheoaks: native Australian flowering trees, also known as casuarinas.

Mandala succulent: native Australian succulent that grows in rings or circles.

The Salt Chronicles, JK (pp.18–24)

This five-part poem has a lyrical tone established through a series of 'I' statements. We should not be too quick to assume that this 'I' is a portrait of Kinsella himself. We can say, however, that the personal voice creates the impression that the poem addresses the reader directly.

1 Aloneness

The poet–speaker describes the isolation of the writing process: 'I realise: so often / I write myself alone / as if no one would go there' (ll.1–3). This anguished and soul-searching persona visits a place others avoid – a landscape of salty residues, an 'environment, where earth-cracks / from the tearing were gateways / to a journey: social / misunderstanding at school, / competitive sport, / rivalry; centre of the earth' (ll.12–17). These fragments and glimpses gesture towards Kinsella's experience. The cracks in the ground are symbolic gateways to a speculative journey deep into the earth's causes and secrets, but the cracks also describe his language, which jumps unevenly from one image to the next. He writes, 'Of myself, I was sure: / the tufts of survivor grass, / the resilient spiked trees / stunted and wind-bent' (ll.24–7), and here the poet's self merges with the natural world. Kinsella explains that his habit of closely observing the places that formed him impelled him to become a writer. He views the environment through the emotional lens of personal experience, feeling and psychobiography (biography of inner life).

2 Salt Wraiths

A wraith is a ghost, or a ghostly image of someone, here cast in salt. One of the ghosts is First Nations folklore: 'dialogues about the feeding of the river / by salt creeks that will drive out the serpent / are persistent' (ll.75–7). Kinsella presents his poetic self as blinded by whiteness: 'it's the wraith's indifference / I missed as a child wandering / the first-degree sunburn / and thinking hallucinations / were prophets or ghosts; in the blaze of white / I lost definitions' (ll.77–82). The white light of the glaring sun, the whiteness of his skin and his cultural whiteness blind him to the full resonance of First Nations myths and histories.

Kinsella references the 'Bradshaw' (l.83), or Gwion Gwion, rock paintings of the Kimberley region. Joseph Bradshaw was a pastoralist who first brought public attention to the paintings in 1891 with his remarkably accurate sketches. Since then, there has been debate over whether the painters were ancestors of the First Nations peoples of the Kimberley or another race altogether. Current consensus is that it was the former. Controversy over the Gwion Gwion paintings continues: since 2009, the Western Australian Government's back-burning program (designed to minimise bushfire risk and facilitate the extraction of gas and oil) has damaged 5000 of the known 8742 sites. Kinsella sees this as the sacrifice of cultural history for mining interests.

3 Mapping and Companionship

Kinsella views mapping as claiming ownership of country. He now sees innocent childhood games as unwitting service to empire: 'my brother and I would go out there in maps / of our ulterior making, and "own" what cousins / "owned" by right of family' (ll.112–14). He records a landscape exploited for farming. The resulting salination is an increasing problem arising from changes in land use and management.

Kinsella writes of 'Diana / perved on from afar by binoculars' (ll.106–7). In Roman mythology Diana was the virgin goddess of hunting and the countryside. The classical poet Ovid describes Diana bathing naked with her maidens after a hunt, when Actaeon the hunter espied her.

Diana splashed him with water, he metamorphosed into a deer and his own dogs hunted and killed him. What does this myth say about Niagara Dam? Colonists described land they had not yet settled or claimed as 'virgin' territory. This notion casts the domineering colonist as male, and as viewing the new territories as passive and female. Kinsella implies that this desire to conquer virgin territory is an abuse of patriarchal (male) privilege, for which men will pay a high price.

4 Contrary

Kinsella observes the use of salt in the US, to melt snow on roads in Ohio (where he worked, at Kenyon College, in the 2000s), and recalls the salt lakes and salination of Western Australia: 'I cannot look at salt / on the crumbling winter roads / of Ohio without it causing / dislocation, a deep disturbance' (ll.126–9). Salt has a mixed legacy: it 'hardens arteries' (l.144) and thus poisons, yet being necessary for life, a 'lack has the shearer crippled' (l.145). It is also mined; indeed, Ohio is well-known for its salt mines.

> The agistment of salt mines
> and the way sweat and blood
> dissolve with history: the paranoia
> that says underneath it all
> must be holes in the text,
> Macherey's unconscious urge to
> see the oppression of salt licks,
> sheep huddled around the drum … (ll.147–54).

These lines gesture to the exploitation involved in salt mining: the 'agistment' process, whereby the corporation pays for the use of the land; and the labour relations, whereby workers expend 'sweat and blood', are forgotten. Kinsella identifies a silence in the historical record, and suggests that this gap explains the political values that drive mining. The reference to 'Macherey' (l.152) is presumably to the French literary critic Pierre Macherey (although the Macherey-Nagel test used to measure salinity is another possible echo). Macherey is a Marxist critic, committed to uncovering elitist class values that shape culture. The idea of a 'political unconscious' suggests that texts repress the struggles that produce them. Kinsella seems to assert that, as a poet, he has a moral obligation to fill those silences and gaps, and to describe the ideologies they mask; that is, to raise awareness of injustices. In this sense his poem affirms Macherey's Marxist political vision. At the end of the above quotation, Kinsella turns to a consideration of the Australian pastoral landscape through the image of 'huddled' sheep.

5 Salt Pans at Dampier: Company Semi-Fact Sheet

This stanza focuses on salt mining in the Dampier region conducted by by mining giant Rio Tinto. The poem jars as it shifts abruptly from lyrical personal poetic language to a seemingly random collection of scientific facts; for example, 'The salt ponds = 100 square kilometres' (l.175).

In the last fourteen lines of the poem Kinsella describes his father's work, without romanticising it or him. As a mine foreman, the poet's father was a member of the management class, and as such he tolerated workers' unionism, but only so far. This is where he and Kinsella differ: 'he tells me this twenty-six / years later – knowing I'd be Union' (ll.191–2). Kinsella, like Macherey (above), is a radical Marxist, opposed to capitalist enterprise and the exploitation of workers and resources to benefit a few. Kinsella seems to imply that it is poetic justice that, in old age, 'the salt drives his [father's] blood pressure, / hijacks his sarcasm' (ll.193–4).

Q How do scientific, personal and poetic discourses clash in this poem?

Key vocabulary

Samphire: coastal plant, native food source, also called sea asparagus.

Fetid: foul-smelling.

Algal: adjective of the noun algae.

Nemesis: arch-enemy, who wilfully causes another's downfall.

Tinnitus: ringing in the ears, due to nerve damage.

Salerium argentium [sic]: the word 'salary', meaning wages, derives from the Latin 'salerium' for salt and 'argentum' for silver; Roman soldiers were paid partly in salt and partly silver.

Dampier: industrial port in the Pilbara, Western Australia, used by mining company Rio Tinto to export iron ore.

Kenworth: brand of transporter or 'the giant salt trucks' (l.188).

Red Lead, Almost Dead, JK (pp.25–6)

Readers of this poem are bombarded with scientific terms, drawn from the poet's work in a laboratory. By beginning 'Led tetroxide bold as ... lead / in the lab, my lab, my phase transition / of poisoned exploration' (ll.1–3), Kinsella makes a 'truth claim': he offers what follows as truths deriving from his knowledge and experience. Only someone with specialised knowledge could question his assertion. The poem meditates on the scientific principles behind mining, the known dangers of the materials unearthed by mining, and everyday uses for those materials.

It is always useful to consider why authors make truth claims. This poem provides a barrage of scientific assertions: that 'lead tetroxide' is used to make stained-glass windows, specifically the 'kookaburra / feature window ... of the gabled / house' (ll.5–7), Australiana typical of the California bungalows built in Australia in the 1920s; that 'the hellzone / of thorium nitrate and mercury' (ll.8–9) is unbelievably dangerous; that liquefied pure lead can be separated but will re-merge when the barrier has been removed, and so forth. The unfolding list of scientific data is oddly punctuated with unscientific concepts such as 'hellzone'; emotive statements, such as 'what's left is the shame' (l.17); and direct addresses to the reader, for example, 'signifier of longevity / you won't enjoy' (ll.23–4). These interpolated (spliced) emotive statements prepare the way for: 'Lead light, lead / unwrapped from yellowcake, the play / of radiation and decay' (ll.20–2), a reference to yellowcake or uranium oxide (ore), which is mined in Western Australia and processed to become dangerously radioactive fuel for nuclear power plants and weapons. Emotion and agency are ascribed to the red lead which 'sits heavy / on the shelf, begging to be mixed / with anything that will change its outlook' (ll.27–9), as though a chemical process psychologically transforms the substances involved.

Q Why does Kinsella compare a chemical process to sheep behaviour?

Key vocabulary

Lead tetroxide: red lead, an ore, or complex chemical compound of oxygen with lead and/or iron, from which iron or lead is extracted.

Selby's: a chemical supply company.

Crucibles: metal or ceramic dishes for smelting metals or other materials.

Bunsen: Bunsen burner, a gas burner that produces a single very hot flame, used in scientific laboratories.

Mettler balance: set of scales for weighing made by Mettler Toledo, manufacturer of precision instruments.

Hydrochloric dissolute: a reference to the chemical process that uses hydrochloric acid to extract iron ore from a compound.

Histories, JK (pp.27–33)

Key quote

> *'My mother taught us respect.*
> *The conversation has never ended.'* (ll.1–2)

This poem is made up of twelve stanzas containing personal memories. It offers a series of snapshots or glimpses rather than a narrative. In stanza 1 the poet–speaker recalls his childhood, helping with refreshments for the farm workers from the Reserve (segregated housing for First Nations peoples). He is shocked that the workers are 'Kids my own age' (l.7).

In stanza 2 he considers the subjective nature of memory; his own memories 'overlap with [his] brother's' (l.12) but are not identical.

In stanza 3 Kinsella reflects upon the craft of writing, and his own stylistic choices. He refers to the imagists, a group of avant-garde (experimental) early-twentieth-century poets. One of the most famous imagists, the American poet Ezra Pound (1885–1972), advocated simple language, vivid rendition of images without emotion, and rejection of traditional poetic conventions. Kinsella states that, whereas the imagists 'cut things back / To bare essentials' (ll.18–19), what he does is 'take the essence of the bush / And make false claims' (ll.20–1). In other words, Kinsella does not strive to represent underlying truths but to create an imaginary world of 'false claims'. He writes, 'I turn a bird into an image, / Co-opt its names' (ll.22–3), stressing that his poetry does not mirror reality. He recasts what he sees, making something new from the raw data of experience. The imagists provide a context and history for Kinsella's verse.

In stanza 4 Kinsella fails to dissuade a group of farm labourers from going shooting, and escapes to Perth. In stanza 5 he recalls writing to a cousin in jail and learning about his Noongar cellmate. In stanza 6 he visits his father and sees 'light in rock' (l.56), that is, fool's gold (iron pyrites). Stanza 7 describes a living room filled with Australian memorabilia, including an emu egg, footy pennants and a painting by the celebrated Western Aranda (Arrernte) artist Albert Namatjira (1902–59) of the Hermannsburg School, which originated at the Hermannsburg Mission in Central Australia. By contrast, stanza 8 describes an American exchange student who talks about race in offensive terms that reflect US race relations, and do not fit the Australian context.

Key point

Kinsella comments self-reflexively: 'Poetry as an artform / Was intended to make up / For what was lost in the taking' (ll.85–7), suggesting that poetry can redress the colonial violation that has shaped Australian history and culture.

In stanza 10 Kinsella arrives in Carnarvon, and meets a boxer. In stanza 11 it seems that someone has given a First Nations man a roof over his head, for which he is grateful. Stanza 12 is a diatribe against mining expressed through odd images and obscure fragments of language. The lines 'the veins / Of the earth / Uprooted' (l.122–4) and 'the earth / Cries out of the dry' (ll.129–30) suggest the land in pain.

Q How does Kinsella respond to Australia's dark history of race relations?

Key vocabulary

Stookers: hay bailers.

Reserve: government-run facility providing housing and rations; a way of controlling First Nations peoples, and separating them from white society.

Smoko: cigarette (or coffee) break.

Mingenew: town north of Perth.

Noongar: First Nations peoples from the WA coastal region, from Geraldton to Esperance.

Rapacious: greedy, plundering.

Golden Gloves: a boxing code.

Mob: First Nations family group.

Vigilantes: people who take the law into their own hands.

Super Pit: mine.

Elegies: poems of lament or mourning.

Hawes – God's Intruder, JK & CPG (pp.34–50)

Key quotes

'Colonised space it became and stayed' (Green, part 6, ll.225)

'The Yamaji architects with the clay and mud huts
Placed on the same land pre settler times
Are forgotten, not talked about, ghosts' (Green, part 10, ll.411–13)

This long co-written dialogical poem in ten parts describes colonial buildings, particularly churches, as a 'whiteworld' (Green, part 2, l.18) that displaced First Nations cultures, histories and peoples. This 'poem of decolonisation' (Kinsella, part 5, l.142) strives to peel back layers of colonial history associated with early-twentieth-century churches designed by the Roman Catholic architect priest Monsignor John Hawes (1876–1956). It focuses on Mullewa's celebrated 'Our Lady of Mt Carmel' (1927), a Romanesque church with the arches and gargoyles characteristic of medieval French buildings, but also Geraldton's 'Big Church' (Green, part 6, l.204). The poets view Hawes' churches as imperial impositions upon 'barna' or First Nations land (Green, part 2, l.15). For his time, Hawes was progressive. Recognising converts' discomfort with worship in European buildings, he offered open-air services at a place known as 'Mass Rock' (Green, part 2, l.25). This site was already a significant Aboriginal cultural site. It had been 'A campsite – home / A place of living / A place of our ceremonies' (Green, part 2, ll.21–3), until the First Nations inhabitants were relocated to one 'Native Mission' or another (Green, part 6, l.213). Green sees this 'Social engineering of our people' as part of the 'colonisers land grab' (part 6, ll.214–15).

Whereas Green gives voice to a history once marginalised, Kinsella describes a system that is brutal on both sides. He recalls being beaten up by a 'white boy' while a 'Yamaji guy' watched (part 7, ll.232–3). When the police asked if any 'black bastards' had been present (l.278), Kinsella said no. Years later the man told him: 'If you hadn't, my whole family / would have paid and would still / be paying' (part 7, ll.296–8). Kinsella and his family are implicated in the colonial system whether they like it or not; he writes, 'We are part of something / we can't quite piece together' (part 5, ll.119–20). At school Kinsella learns white history, beginning with the explorer George Grey (1812–98), but writes, 'that wasn't part of my vision, though later I'd rewrite it / as a poem of decolonisation' (part 5, ll.140–2). He rejects the colonial system of endemic conflict fuelled by racist ignorance and greed. Looking to the future, he writes, 'When I return to Geraldton, / to what part of me is there, ... I listen / hoping my errors / will find redress' (part 5, ll.143–4, 150–2).

Q What unites the poets' distinct voices in this poem?

Bottlebrush Behind Our Lady of Fatima Church, Nanson, Chapman Valley, JK (pp.51–2)

This poem and its pair, Green's 'Honey to Lips Bottlebrush', comment on the preceding poem, 'Hawes – God's Intruder'. The three poems are linked. Kinsella reflects on the collaborative experience of 'working with Charmaine / on this array of monuments tapped into the region, such / concentrations of God' (ll.5–7). He situates monuments, such as the churches, in terms of geographic location, family histories, local fauna and flora, farming and 'the ECHELON communications base / playing realpolitik lies' (ll.13–14). ECHELON is a surveillance program operated by the US in agreement with Australia, New Zealand, Canada and the UK, with an Australian Defence Satellite Communications ground station in Geraldton.

Kinsella declares this combination of personal, historical, and institutional elements to be 'Surreal' and 'uncanny' (ll.17, 19). He reflects upon his own words, observing that each is a 'trendy, easy word' (l.17) that 'insists on being spoken, an intrusion that sends / the bungarra [goanna] shooting off into the scrub' (ll.19–20). He suggests that English, the colonisers' tongue, is deeply implicated in the violence done to the region. This is obscured when men such as Hawes are celebrated. The poem has an interesting structure: it comprises twenty-four lines broken into eight three-line stanzas, each joined by a sentence that runs across the break between the stanzas. This run-over sentence means that the stanza breaks are visual rather than semantic (relating to meaning). The visual formality of the poem's structure is in tension with its conversational language.

Q What does Kinsella mean by histories that 'resonate in deadly ways' (l.5)?

Key vocabulary

Shriven: presented to a priest for confession, penance or absolution (archaic).

Realpolitik: political policy based on power rather than on ideals.

Honey to Lips Bottlebrush, CPG (pp.53–4)

In the opening couplet, 'Young teachings perched on Walkaway hill / Space reclaiming decolonising respacing' (ll.1–2), Green highlights her rescripting of the colonial legacy. This poem challenges once-dominant values and narratives. She focuses on Hawes' legacy: 'Appetite not here for Hawes' mudpie / Young thirst for knowledge Yamaji' (ll.10–11). That youthful thirst for knowledge is satisfied by 'Sucking nectar bottlebrush sweet' (l.16), taking nourishment from the landscape and flora, and recovering First Nations histories: 'Dance ground feet sand reunite connect / Still wind still ancestors come to visit' (ll.25–6). This twenty-nine-line poem is structured with four-line verses interspersed with indented italicised segments of uneven length. The indented segments open with the title of the poem, 'Honey to lips bottlebrush', and close with '*Not on this land not here*'; repetition gives a chorus effect.

Q What does Green mean by 'Wheat grain money worshipped' (ll.23–4)?

Our Lady of Mt Carmel, Mullewa, JK (pp.55–6)

The poem opens with an epigraph stating Hawes' 'great affinity with the Aboriginal people of Mullewa', taken from www.monsignorhawes.com.au. The poem undercuts the celebratory tone of the epigraph. It is made up of four six-line stanzas and a fifth three-line stanza. Each begins,

'We had to go home that way', emphasising the concepts of 'home' and local identity. Kinsella does not see Hawes as a sympathetic man who enriched the culture of the area, as the website declares. He asserts, 'Mullewa / *isn't* the church, but the place where people live / across many conversations, and country isn't a cross' (ll.3–5).

Kinsella perceives that Hawes is celebrated at the expense of other stories that define the region, such as the famous 'wreath flowers' that attract 'the wildflower visitors' (ll.9, 10) each spring. In spite of the tourists, 'fencers have taken / out so much of the roadside vegetation' (ll.10–11) and the wreath flowers are compromised. Nonetheless, travelling across the 'stony ground' (l.15) Kinsella observes what binds the community together: '*inland inland* following railway, road trains, the mucking / around in the school playground. All of that / making the town, community' (ll.16–18). By contrast he views the church as a sinister 'caricature Romanesque tower – colonial theatre / of cruelty' (ll.21–2). In the closing lines, 'We had to go back home that way, wondering / about the legacy of architecture, the caretaking / of affinity' (ll.25–7), Kinsella questions the values that are nourished and maintained through the caretaking of structures built on colonial exploitation.

Key vocabulary

Romanesque: medieval architectural style, with semicircular arches above columns.

No other road, CPG (pp.57–8)

Key quote

'Man-made temple like peacock stands
Marker of a civilised yet uncivilised world
A space for those to pray their sins away ' (ll.20–2)

In an echo of Kinsella's 'Our Lady of Mt Carmel, Mullewa', Green's poem repeats the line, 'Home is back that way, there is no other' (l.1). The poem's three stanzas of uneven length alternate with a strident three-line chorus: 'Mass Rock is the intruder in our space / Mass Rock is not my significant site / My people's campsite not Hawes' space' (ll.16–18), alluding to the site's earlier history. Green describes the church as built for show; it embodies the hypocrisy of the colonists. Mass Rock is where Hawes conducted open-air services for First Nations converts to Catholicism. Green contests the meaning of certain locations, and reasserts the histories of her people.

Q What are 'civilised colonial pagans with gargoyle guards' (l.24)?

Key vocabulary

Gargoyle: a rainwater spout in the form of a grotesque head with open mouth; a feature of medieval cathedrals.

I don't like flying over, CPG (p.59)

Key quote

'This is not a holiday island
It's a prison memory of shootings
Hangings, drownings, measles, influenza' (ll.13–15)

Green exposes the dark history of Wadjemup (Rottnest Island) as a place where First Nations peoples were imprisoned and died. She pays tribute to her kinsfolk: 'We must continue to remember / To honour the men who died out there' (ll.18–19).

Q Why is it important to recall 'cruel colonial practices' (l.16)?

Wildflower Singing, CPG (p.60)

Green celebrates First Nations history and culture, 'Like a feast laid out' (l.1) in front of her. Sight and sound mix, as she regards her 'Ancestral lands / Singing in wildflowers' (ll.6–7). This simple poem is a positive affirmation of traditions kept alive by the lands themselves, and of Green's poetry.

Culture Bath, CPG (p.61)

This short instructional poem is written in a familiar but imperative voice; it gives the impression that the speaker is advising a First Nations friend. Green seeks to jolt her kinsfolk out of passivity. Each individual has a responsibility to actively engage with their heritage: 'Let it wash over you' (l.2), she writes. In a firm encouraging tone, she urges: 'Don't look the other way / Don't be an observer / Embrace your culture with open arms / For it is your belonging' (ll.11–14).

Q 'Culture Bath' is written for a First Nations Australian readership. How do you react?

I won't pretend, CPG (p.62)

In this short poem Green addresses the difficulties of 'Living in an intercultural space' (l.2). There are inevitable 'Cultural clashes and tensions' (l.3), but it is 'Inspiring – rewarding' (l.12). The way forward is 'Finding time to walk over / Each other's barna' (ll.16–17), that is, respectfully engaging with each culture's traditions, places and histories.

Q What role does poetry play in making intercultural life a success?

Campfire, CPG (p.63)

This poem concerns cultural exchange between 'First Peoples' (l.16) of Australia and New Zealand: 'We share this space / Yamaji to Maori to Yamaji' (ll.6–7). According to Green, this 'sharing' of place and culture is unusual: 'In other parts of Australia / The youth fight each other' (ll.10–11). This occurs when First Nations peoples turn their backs on their culture and 'take on attitudes of White Australia' (l.14).

Q What does Green think Maori and Yamaji share?

Tangi, CPG (pp.64–5)

'Tangi' is the Maori word for funeral. Green comforts a Maori friend whose mother has died. The locus (place) of this poem is the 'land of the long white cloud' (l.32), New Zealand. Her friend takes her mother's body home to her family, 'Before her final journey from physical world' (l.12). Green repeats that this is 'not our way' (ll.4, 37).

Q Why does the speaker find the Maori tangi unsettling?

Yamaji Culture, CPG (pp.66–7)

Green affirms that 'Yamaji culture' is 'worth loving' (l.2), 'worth fighting for' (l.3) and 'worth being loved' (ll.4). The speaker asks an unnamed, apparently hostile, interlocutor: 'Why tell me I don't need it?' (l.5). Concerned about Yamaji abandoning their cultural roots, she tells them: 'Don't crawl into a / Dark corner of cultural nothingness' (ll.16–17). Injecting a note of hope, she writes, 'I watch Yamaji culture change / It adapts to survive' (ll.25–6).

Q Green urges, 'Hang on – hang on tight countrymen / To our Yamaji Culture' (ll.34–5). How is this to be achieved?

Lake Magic Resonances (January 2017), JK (pp.68–76)

This thirteen-stanza poem is dedicated to Kinsella's friend and fellow academic, Tony Hughes-d'Aeth, Professor of Australian literature at the University of Western Australia, who has reviewed Kinsella's books. The locus of this poem is Lake Magic, an inland lake southeast of Perth. This difficult poem does not readily give its secrets to the reader. Each stanza presents an abstract, rather than a realist, document of the poet–speaker's psychological response to a place.

Stanza 1 creates a surreal impression through seemingly unrelated statements layered in a bricolage (assemblage) of words and sentence fragments. For example, unexpected transitions are made from 'summer's flameless burn of night' (l.1) to salt residues, to no (phone) reception, to 'hope rises into darkness' (l.5). Stanza 2 continues in this vein. The couplet 'White branchings / up out of the bed of lack' (ll.8–9), for example, could describe white cracks in the surface of the dry salt bed, but the idea of a 'bed of lack' is evocative without being precise. When the poet–speaker asks, 'what is being said, what is being said?' (l.15), the poem gives voice to a reader's likely response to this abstract writing.

Stanza 3 jumps from 'backyard radiation' (l.20) to 'ornate / rock dragons' (ll.25–6): lizards, endemic to Western Australia, that watch the poet–speaker as he climbs through the arid landscape. Stanza 4 is headed 'Draining from Lake King'. On one level, it concerns the water system associated with Lake Magic, including Lake King and the Camm River, but, on the other, it tends towards abstraction. Warped imagery, such as 'rock looming / and its lizard eyes taking / in so much salt' (ll.33–5) makes the reader question whether the lizards mentioned in stanza 3 were real, or imagined by the poet–speaker.

Stanza 5 names the dreamscape established so far: 'electrolytes of psyche / and weirdness of sleeping' (ll.40–1). Electrolytes are chemical substances that conduct electricity. This odd juxtaposition describes the poem. The nightmare continues in stanza 6, with water that cannot be drunk, perhaps because it is a mirage, and stanza 7's inland sea with imagined ships. The description of the landscape in stanza 8, headed with the question 'Who to blame?', is punctuated by a '*Vut vut*!' (ll.83, 89,106) noise, as if the birds were making comment. This echoes the strange 'Jug jug jug jug jug jug' birdsong that interrupts TS Eliot's abstract descriptions of the 'unreal city' in his famous, but notoriously difficult, modernist poem 'The Wasteland' (1921). As in Eliot's poem, the poet–speaker's control over language dissolves and he questions his own existence: 'I lake, I make lake of me / when I really shouldn't' (ll.90–1).

After a three-line 'Interlude' in which Kinsella wonders how his wife and son would respond to this landscape, in stanza 9, headed 'I refuse', he asserts, 'I refuse to bend to form / or to a prosody of certainty / when all is vicarious' (ll.110–12). Here 'form' refers to the shape of the poem, and 'prosody' (rhythm, stress, intonation of speech) to words; he suggests that his poem does not use language or poetic structure to create 'certainty' or clarity, because 'all is vicarious'. Vicarious literally means communication with God filtered through a 'vicar' (from the Latin word for 'substitute'). This suggests that nothing about the world can be known with certainty because our knowledge of it is second-hand.

Stanza 10 focuses on a young couple visiting the salt lake. Stanza 11 involves further impossible abstractions such as, 'I count syllables of salt' (l.137). The poet–speaker finds language and landscape inseparable. In stanza 12 he advocates looking at First Nations rock art without western European 'colonial' (l.156) eyes, and imagines a rock lizard speaks to him. Stanza 13 closes with non-specific instructions such as 'Stay clear' (l.164) – but of what?, the reader wonders – and then ends with the birdsong established earlier, '*Vut vut*! / *Vut vut*! / *Vut vut*!' (ll.169–71).

Q What does the poem suggest about the poet–speaker's state of mind?

Key vocabulary

Gnamma: waterhole.

Hydrography: the science of measuring and mapping bodies of water.

Lee: area sheltered from wind.

Gypsum: soft white or grey mineral deposit.

Polyphony: multiple parts combined in a piece of music.

Crystallography: scientific study of crystals.

Paleochannel: remnant of an inactive river.

The Artlessness of Internal Travel, JK (pp.77–81)

This poem of thirteen unnumbered stanzas describes travel within inland Western Australia. Specific places are named – 'The Canning River fed Bull Creek' (l.3), 'the Chapman River'; (l.8), 'the Pilbara' (l.20), and 'Carnarvon Whaling Station' (l.108) – but the focus is on what travel *means*. Philosophical probing begins with the opening: 'Going away enforced where I was. / There was no here without there' (ll.1–2). The poet examines how his personal identity has been affected by mobility and relocation. People travel to be refreshed by a scenery change, but they carry emotional baggage wherever they go. This point is made through a personal example: 'Always heading Down South / or Up North, a thread through / a broken marriage' (ll.13–15). Travel is no escape from his mental landscape; he seems to recall travel between Perth and Mullewa necessitated by his parents' broken marriage.

The poem stresses that humans coexist with the places they inhabit and visit. At some points the speaker seems to merge with the physical landscape: for example, 'I am still there, scant vegetation / and presence I can now explain' (ll.48–9). What he describes seems unreal, like a hallucination or dream, and he is 'alone and lost' (l.44). His words have no permanence: 'In whose footsteps / I follow, and the marks I leave behind: so distinct, / but empty, the yellowing spray-fringe at the edges' (ll.90–2). But whose footsteps is he following: the 'wodjil' (acacia), the 'rock dragons' (lizards), or the poet Frank O'Hara, mentioned in the ninth stanza?

Key vocabulary

The Scarp: Australian slang for 'escarpment'.

Jarrah: Australian hardwood, eucalypt (gum tree) native to WA.

Golden Fleece: Australian petroleum company active 1893–1981, whose logo, a yellow ram, was displayed on petrol stations across the country.

Wodjil: tall shrubby vegetation dominated by acacia.

Karri: (red) eucalyptus tree.

Tuart: (white) eucalyptus tree.

Edges of Aridity, JK (pp.82–4)

The locus of this poem is the northern Flinders Ranges in South Australia, the traditional lands of the Adnyamathanha people to whom the poem is dedicated. This is an arid region through which water runs occasionally, where river red gums and native pines grow, and a 'whirly whirly' (l.24) (or willy-willy: a dusty, spiralling wind that occurs when hot and cold air masses meet) passes through. The landscape is a backdrop for profound questions about the meaning of existence. It asks what separates two states of being: town and country, life and death. The line between a town and a mine shifts quickly to the flimsy line between life and death: 'Out of this, the cemetery is an edge I know – it speaks / to all places of the dead, inside and out' (ll.21–2). This is reinforced by evocative word pictures, such as 'headstones bled of script' (l.36), which gesture to the violence of language. The poet is haunted by the overwhelming presence of 'the dead' who 'are loud in their graves (l.46); he realises that 'Edges are beginnings, not ends' (l.47). This repeated statement underscores the cyclical nature of life. The poet–speaker guides the reader through consideration of death towards the hope of natural renewal and affirmation: 'the needles of acacias and their seedpods / opening, hoping new growth will join old, / and know these edges are beginnings, not ends' (ll.51–3).

Q What does an edge suggest in this poem?

Key vocabulary

Cassia: shrub with yellow flowers.

Wedge-taileds: wedge-tailed eagles, birds of prey.

Simulacra: unreal appearance.

Slag heap: mining refuse.

Reconstruction of the *Foundation of Perth 1829*, Painted by George Pitt Morison for the Centenary of 1929: a poem against ekphrasis, JK (pp.85–8)

This poem concerns the painting *Foundation of Perth 1829* (1929), a historical reconstruction of the founding of Perth, painted by George Pitt Morison (1861–1946), a hundred years after the events depicted. Kinsella denounces the painting for its triumphant account of settler–colonial history, writing: 'favours are done / in the retelling: the centennial / picture confirms what they / want, what they've always / known' (ll.63–7). This is a clear rejection of the kinds of history, storytelling and art that prop up the myth of white settlement and terra nullius (the idea that the land was owned by no one when Europeans arrived). This inference is underscored by the dedication of the poem to Kim Scott (b. 1957), the Noongar writer whose award-winning historical novel *That Deadman Dance* (2010) describes European settlement from a Noongar perspective. Kinsella offers Scott's writing as the antithesis to Morison's painting.

Q What is the importance of 'retelling' (l.63) in this poem?

Key vocabulary

Queen Mary: (1867–1953), wife of Britain's King George V, queen consort 1910–36.

Mrs Dance: Helen Dance, wife of William Dance, commander of the sloop HMS Sulphur.

Captain Stirling: Sir James Stirling (1791–1865), Scottish naval officer and colonial administrator; founded Perth (and Freemantle) on the Swan River; first Governor of Western Australia.

Xanthorrhoeas: native grass trees.

Zamias: species of palm tree indigenous to Western Australia.

Herbariums: collections of (dried) plant specimens.

Ficus trees: fig trees.

Sulphur: one of two ships carrying the first European settlers to Australia.

Respect, JK (pp.89–90)

Key quote

'... the protector rounded up people like songs of praise ...' (ll.35–6)

This is Kinsella's account of a trip he made to see his mother at 'Wendy's place' (l.15) with a First Nations friend of his mother. The opening – 'Mum's friend says that her people / know which of the white families in the district / behaved decently' (ll.1–3) – asks how the past shapes the present: 'the sins / of the past are as much the sins of now / as of the future' (ll.6–8).

Past actions caused the salination of waterways, leaving 'the rainbow serpent choked up' (l.9), a 'dead river' (l.14). Kinsella and his mother's friend follow 'the annealed / path of the serpent' (ll.20–1). First Nations history (represented by the serpent's path) joins with the white history of 'farmland, scars through the surveyor's mapping' (ll.22) in 'cauterised antiphony' (l.21). Cauterise means to burn skin or flesh to stop bleeding and antiphony is dialogue between two groups of singers or instruments. Kinsella links this aural and visual image of two choirs singing music burnt into the land to Australia's violent history of appropriation and dispossession, justified by religious ideals.

Kinsella describes a place with both First Nations and settler history. He renounces the privilege of his own whiteness – 'Any rights I have over words I cede to you' (l.48) – but it is unclear whether 'you' is the landscape, his mother, his mother's friend or the original inhabitants of the land.

Q What does the phrase 'electroshock of myth inversion' (l.45) suggest?

Key vocabulary

Annealed: toughened; glass heated then slowly cooled, to strengthen it.

Nganayungu Yagu, CPG (p.91)

In this simple poem of praise, Green writes about her mother, Yagu. Yagu instilled pride in her daughter, telling her to 'Walk tall and strong' (l.5) and assuring her, 'Your ancestors' spirits / Will protect you' (ll.14–15). Green believes, 'Her spirit watches / Over me / As I move around / On this our land' (ll.23–6).

Q How does Green's 'Nganayungu Yagu' answer Kinsella's 'Respect'?

Rain Clouds' Arrival, CPG (p.92)

Green celebrates rain that renews a natural 'cycle of growth' (l.9). It nourishes the relationship between land and its human occupants: 'Refreshing and sustaining / Tracks and memories / Across the land' (ll.18–20).

Q How does this poem define 'Nature's way' (l.5)?

Lake Joondalup, CPG (p.93)

There is some anger and resentment in the opening couplet of this poem concerning urban encroachment upon places that were once wild: 'Suburban disturbance / Rooftops hurting the eye' (ll.1–2). The poet–speaker experiences displacement as she watches birds at the water's edge. The poem concludes wistfully, as 'Lake Joondalup / Waits for its people' (ll.21–2).

Q What does Green mean by 'Coloniser's villages' (l.5)?

Old Girl, CPG (pp.94–5)

The poem is dedicated to Julie Dowling, a Badimaya First Nations painter and activist who describes herself as engaging in decolonisation. She paints figurative works in a social-realist style (associated with Mexican painters Frida Kahlo and Diego Rivera). Her paintings are held in major art collections across Australia. In an example of ekphrasis, Green describes Dowling's painting of a First Nations woman: 'Old Girl's eyes draw me on first sight / Pulling me close into her presence / I know Old Girl I seen her before / My Aunty, my Nanna, my Cousin' (ll.1–4). Dowling's painting, *Old Girl*, represents a woman who witnessed 'the / Coloniser's cruel practices' (ll.7–8) and 'Yet Old Girl Stands firm' (l.9). Green celebrates Dowling's efforts to redefine art by shifting away from white and colonial subjects towards images that undercut 'the harshness of the world' (l.34).

Q How does Green think art can help to create a more positive future?

Blue Scar, CPG (p.96)

Green depicts roads as blue scars on traditional land. This colonial imposition 'Does not cancel out or replace / Beliefs, customs or values' (ll.9–10); they live on and adapt 'To remind you of / The strength and resilience / Of a people belonging' (ll.15–17).

Q How does Green balance the past with hope for the future in this poem?

Simply Yarning, CPG (p.97)

Through the dedication to Dawn Bessarab, a Bard/Yjindjabandi woman from the West Kimberley region of WA, Green signals her engagement with current academic discussions about inclusivity and mutual respect. See more discussion in the 'Themes, ideas & values' section (pp.60–7).

Yarn Response Poem, JK (pp.98–9)

This is Kinsella's response to Green's 'Simply Yarning', expressing shared values and his engagement with Yamaji culture. See more discussion in the 'Themes, ideas & values' section (pp.60–7).

Third Space, CPG (pp.100–1)

The poem opens with 'Come grab my mara' (l.1). 'Mara' means 'hand'; this is an invitation to enter cross-cultural dialogue and to embrace 'diversity' (l.4). Green tells her white interlocutor that, to create something new together, both must 'discard our / Protective robes' (ll.32–3), or prejudices and biases.

Key point

Green emphasises that openness will be needed on both sides for reconciliation between white settlers and First Nations peoples.

Ngana Nyinda, CPG (p.102)

The Wajarri title means, 'Who are you?' The poem captures the language of Aboriginal speakers asking questions to gauge cultural and familial context.

Q What is the effect of repeating 'Ngana Nyinda' in the poem?

Balayi Mundungu, CPG (pp.103–4)

The Glossary (pp.146–7) translates 'Balayi' as 'beware' and Mundungu are evil spirits or 'little devils ... Whispering in your ears ... When someone different / Strolls by or steps into / Your little yard' (ll.3,6, 8–10). They pollute 'common ground' and 'bring out your / Prejudices' (ll.25, 27–8). The poem is about minimising negative, destructive thoughts in order to build a positive future.

Q What hope for the future does Green express in this poem?

On Julie Dowling's *My White Friend*, Geraldton Regional Gallery, 2017, JK (p.105)

Kinsella describes a painting by Julie Dowling (another example of ekphrasis). An italicised couplet opens and closes the poem: '*Who do we work for? Who pays up, smiling, friendly-like? / Who has washed and ironed the linen dresses? The altar cloth?*' (ll.1–2). The reader is prompted to consider the economic system established by colonialism in Australia: where does our money really come from? Who did the work? Did the 'white friend' profit from that exploitation? While the italicised lines seem to represent the voice of the white friend, the body of the poem documents Kinsella's response to the painting. It analyses the imagery in the painting; for example, 'the church' initiates reflection on religious concepts such as 'eternity' (l.3), what it means to 'be good spirit' (l.6), 'truth' (l.7) and the nature of real friendship. The white friend's feet disappear among 'introduced grasses, native grasses' (l.5); this is an image of contemporary Australian society made up of First Nations peoples, cultures and traditions and introduced western, European, white ones.

Q How does the poem's interrogative (questioning) tone affect the reader?

The Great Western Woodlands, JK (pp.106–7)

The poem is dedicated to Sister Veronica Brady (1929–2005), an Australian literature scholar at the University of Western Australia. Kinsella recalls a visit to the Victorian Mallee, a landscape dramatically changed by farming, describing 'the emptiness / of grassed plains that weren't / grassed plains' (ll.7–9). This environmental degradation makes him think about a Western Australian landscape: 'the essence of the

Western / woodlands is clarified' (ll.11–12). He continues, 'Its loss would be / an act of terror' (ll.13–14). The woodland plants are sentient (feeling) beings: the quandong (a small tree with edible red fruit) 'wants its own space, / gets on well with its neighbours' (ll.24–5). Animals inhabit the landscape with purpose: an emu, a roo, an eagle and an ant 'are going somewhere, / having somewhere to go. / This is more than human / intuition' (ll.35–8). The landscape is sentient too; it is 'This great lung, / this great mind ... it is the everything we are' (ll.44–5, 51).

Key vocabulary

Dundas mahogany: Eucalyptus brockwayi, a gum tree endemic to Western Australia.

Blue Hazmat Suits in the Coolbellup Bush Prior to its Destruction, JK (pp.108–9)

Key quote

> 'a consummate piece of pastoral diplomacy
> played out on crown land, a colonial
> power trip ...' (ll.8–10)

This bitter protest poem concerns asbestos contamination in a nature reserve in Coolbellup, a suburb of Perth. The asbestos was disturbed when the Roe highway was built in 2017. Kinsella's father-in-law, his wife Tracy's father, breathed in asbestos fibres and is now dying of asbestosis. Bitterly Kinsella describes 'A parody of deaths from blue asbestos' (l.2) caused by 'sadists' (l.6). When asbestos was discovered, 'blue hazmat suits are seen / bobbing in and out of the undergrowth' (ll.6–7). Then 'the arrests mount and fibres fall out' (ll.14). He rails at the 'smug capitalist[s]' (l.29) whose 'rowdy machines' (l.32) caused the fibres to be 'dispersed among loved ones' (l.36).

Kinsella writes of 'pastoral diplomacy' (l.8). Pastoral means related to farming (in the sense of pastures), but also the care a church minister, priest or pastor provides to a congregation. Both meanings suggest that the profit-driven ethos of colonialism, justified by religion, continues to devastate innocent people. After 'diplomacy' there is a stanza break, although the sentence itself continues. This visual disruption of the sentence without altering the syntax (word order within a sentence), reminds the reader of the deep cracks that fracture the scene described.

Q Kinsella declares angrily, 'Children breathe here, you bastards' (l.28). What is the effect of this hostility?

Cathedral Avenue, JK (p.110)

The word 'Cathedral' highlights the poem's religious theme, while 'Avenue' conjures an avenue of trees. The opening lines, 'This doesn't have to be a requiem, / no, not yet' (ll.1–2) tell us that the poem is not a mass for the dead. The 'not yet' warns readers to treasure the natural world of trees (salmon gums and wandoo) before it is too late. Kinsella describes the trees as sentient beings that breathe. They have a symbiotic (co-dependent) relationship with humans: 'Each breath these strong / old trees let us have is a breath that keeps / us going' (ll.2–4). He writes, 'The branches reach to hold / the sky in place to keep / earth and sky connected' (ll.7–9) – their branches hold our world together; and they connect 'Prayers in all languages / and all faiths' (ll.10–11). Kinsella invites readers to see religiosity in nature. Trees are part of an ecosystem upon which all living creatures depend, but 'which the machinery would cut short' (l.20).

Q What do the trees tell us in this poem?

Sammies (Salmon Gums), JK (pp.111–13)

This poem concerns the felling of salmon gums, which Kinsella also calls 'sammies' or 'Wurak'. The opening line, *'And so the salmon gums are killed off'* (l.1), suggests that this is the requiem (funeral mass) that the preceding poem anticipated. Kinsella observes ancient salmon gums that have witnessed 'the changes of timeline owned and owning' (l.8), but are now cordoned off with 'plastic ribbons' (l.12). Their 'deletion diminishes you, never mind / country itself' (ll.21–2). The poet views the trees as sentient and architectural: 'Hands reaching / to touch, a nest high above makes glyphs. / Sammies, poured into their columns, / ribbed vaults, horizons of canopy / through which land and sky parley' (ll.26–30).

Kinsella compares the destruction of the trees to a bushfire ignited by an unthinking passer-by: 'Always / these paradoxes like cigarettes ashed out of car / windows at the height of summer, flickers / of holocaust in such a casual gesture' (ll.51–3). The reference to the World War II Holocaust, during which millions of Jews were murdered, casts dark associations onto the destruction of a local environment and the knowledge and culture of First Nations peoples.

Q Why does Kinsella think Aboriginal people have more to grieve than he does?

Key vocabulary

Glyph: an ornamental groove or channel.

Scry: foretell.

Still Shame – Why?, CPG (p.114)

This represents a dialogue between two Yamaji people: one is 'Too shame to dance' (l.1) and the other affirms, 'This world needs to / See all beautiful Yamaji' culture (ll.12–13). It blends English and Yamaji words to capture the language of contemporary Yamaji speakers.

Q What is the effect on readers of the expression of two positions in this dialogue poem?

Strong Wajarri Man, CPG (p.115)

Key quote

> '... some now say no to this Wajarri man
> For Wajarri land he can't care' (ll.15–16)

Like the previous poem, here English and Wajarri words are blended to describe a seventy-year-old man who identifies as Wajarri, although 'His skin is fair – no argument there' (l.1). This line is repeated. Although he was 'raised in town' (l.5), his family can trace 'kin, place, country' (l.7). Green asserts that Wajarri living on their 'barna' (land) have a responsibility to include urban members in their community.

Q How does the speaker view tensions within the Yamaji community?

Identity Police, CPG (p.116)

Tackling negative attitudes towards 'fair skinned Yamaji' (l.7), this poem is addressed to 'Mr Mrs Identity Police' (l.2), that is, to Yamaji who judge others' credentials. The poet–speaker warns that, in time, their 'Grand kids, great grandkids' (l.11) may face similar judgements.

Q Which words might the addressee come to 'regret' (l.25)?

Drug Slaves, CPG (p.117)

Green comments on the drug problems plaguing contemporary First Nations communities. The poet–speaker criticises dealers and drug couriers, 'who give the first shot / The ones who give the first taste / To our beautiful healthy strong young ones' (ll.7–9). Such people even exploit their own family members.

Q What does the phrase 'broken minds' suggest (l.23)?

Needle Teacher, CPG (p.118)

The poem's title plays on and subverts the usual conception of teachers as helpful individuals who enrich the lives of others. The 'needle teacher' (l.17) of this poem who introduces others to intravenous drug use is 'The wicked witch of the speed world' (l.18).

Dark Light Bulbs, CPG (pp.119–20)

The 'dark light' of the title is an oxymoron (seemingly self-contradictory figure of speech) that describes 'A sinister dark side' (l.7) of the drug culture destroying First Nations communities. The 'dark' purpose to which light bulbs are put is as makeshift drug-smoking devices.

Q What does Green mean by 'a tool to hell' (l.8)?

Death Stress, CPG (pp.121–2)

Green describes the trauma of death within her community. The causes of death differ, but the impact is the focus here. What matters is the loss: 'They will no longer tread / Upon the soft earth with you' (ll.17–18). Her community is emotionally overloaded: 'We suffer death stress / We grieve for ourselves as well' (ll.40–1).

Q What does Green say about 'that gut wrenching feeling of death' (l.1)?

Funeral Directors, CPG (p.123)

The theme of death in 'Death Stress', 'Dark Light Bulbs', 'Needle Teacher' and 'Drug Slaves' is continued in this poem. It discusses how contemporary First Nations peoples develop new rituals. Green compares 'real funeral directors' whose job is to be 'kind / Patient, sympathetic, respectful' (ll.4–5), with Yagu, her mother, who is an 'unofficial funeral planner' (l.19). Yagu wants to 'decolonise funeral ceremony' (l.15) to acknowledge First Nations cultures. And after 'stressful but respectful' (l.18) conversation with the official funeral directors, she succeeds.

Q Why is 'stressful but respectful' (l.18) dialogue necessary?

Monitoring Lizards, CPG (p.124)

The poet–speaker mentions First Nations peoples paid by white people to monitor lizards, clear land and assist with 'Heritage site clearances' (l.10). This work is a 'trap for the poor' (l.11). It 'Will bring some food, grog and gunja' (marijuana) (l.16), so they cannot refuse it, but 'Monitoring for the robbers / And their false plans' (ll.19–20) entrenches disadvantage.

Q How does Green see First Nations peoples as complicit in their own disadvantage?

A New Ode to Westralia: Anthem for All Future Sporting Events, JK (pp.125–6)

Key quote

'... Poets of the world, take notice. They will
    close
you down the moment you break free of your anthologies,
your safety in pages of literary journals, the comforts
of award nights.' (ll.13–17)

The title references 'Ode to Westralia', an anonymous satirical poem published in the Kalgoorlie Sun in April 1899. It begins: 'Land of Forests, fleas, and flies, / Blighted hopes and blighted eyes, / Art thou hell in earth's disguise, / Westralia?' This indictment of the colony was widely imitated. Kinsella's poem is a sporting anthem, suggesting that it is celebratory and patriotic, but the reference to the 1899 ode suggests that it is a satire (a sarcastic, humorous critique).

Like the earlier poem, Kinsella's 'A New Ode to Westralia' exudes disgust and frustration, but his opening line, 'The state is killing our souls' (l.1) lacks the humour of its predecessor. The poet–speaker asserts that the state has 'murdered the people' (l.2) and propagated 'destruction' (l.6). Kinsella's critique of Western Australia is direct, impassioned and even belligerent about government policy. The lines 'The state has deployed vicious antibodies to kill the good cells / and let the infection thrive' (l.4–5) invoke the ancient idea of the body politic, a corporal (bodily) analogy which imagines the state as a living body with the monarch (or head of state) as the head, and the people making up the other parts. This concept naturalised the idea that the head of state was the rational part of the body. It was used to justify the state's absolute power over the people, and ruthless and violent means of maintaining that power. For example, only the head could recognise that a limb was corrupt and know when to cut it off. The body could survive without a limb, but not without a head.

Kinsella has this in mind when he addresses the state's control of language. The poem issues an urgent call to expose the truth of the state's systemic brutality. He writes: 'The state has no intention of letting traditional owners maintain / traditional / places of worship of culture or belonging – it's always been / about / the twin poles of denial and deletion' (ll.24–8). It is also responsible for the destruction of native flora and fauna.

Q Would this poem suit a sporting event? Explain your answer.

Key vocabulary

Plato's theory of forms: the idea that physical forms are shadows of true reality, proposed in Plato's *The Republic,* where he outlines an ideal political state. The fact that Plato excluded poets from his republic because poets deal in invention and not truth may explain Kinsella's hostility.

Gung-ho: unthinkingly enthusiastic (here, for war).

Always thieves, CPG (pp.127–8)

Key quote

'Massacres were strategic for any interference
This my friend is how White Australia did it
This my friend is Australia's history' (ll.19–21)

The title of *False Claims of Colonial Thieves* comes from this poem by Green on the body politic. The bitter truth-telling begins: 'Thieves arrived in all disguises / Colonial officers, convicts, settlers, free men' (ll.1–2), a pointed attack on the British colonial system imposed upon her people.

Key point

Green points her finger at the legal justification of the 'colonial thieves' (l.7): 'Thieves wrapped warmly with the / Blankets of terra nullius' (ll.5–6). This principle justified 'A bloodied history worthy of thieves' (l.12) and it persists: 'Thieves remain' (l.24) and corporations, businesses and governments have 'Dirty hands coated with traces of blood' (ll.27).

Q How does this poem sum up the collection as a whole?

In Marapikurrinya: for Ms Dhu, JK (pp.129–30)

'Ms Dhu' is a Yamaji woman who died in custody in 2014 in Marapikurrinya (South Hedland, Western Australia). Ms Dhu's real name was withheld out of respect. She was arrested for unpaid fines, and then subjected to inhumane treatment. When she became ill, doctors and prison guards assumed that she was experiencing drug withdrawal symptoms and did not take her suffering seriously. In 2016 a coronial inquiry delivered an indictment of the policy of incarcerating people for failure to pay fines. A video was released, showing Ms Dhu writhing in pain. As no perpetrators were named, Ms Dhu's family and supporters felt that justice was denied. More recently, the Black Lives Matter movement in Australia brought public attention to her death.

This poem protests the shameful record of Aboriginal deaths in custody in Australia. Kinsella dedicates the poem to 'Ms Dhu' to ensure that her memory would 'outlive' (l.41) her oppressors.

Q What kind of reaction does this poem provoke?

Growing, CPG (p.131)

The speaker of this short poem describes herself as a caterpillar 'Far too long cocooned' who 'Waited patiently for the wings' (ll.2, 4). This simile is extended: those who never grow wings 'will surely kill us' (l.12).

Q What is the significance of the caterpillar?

Shopping Centre Carpark, JK (pp.132–3)

An everyday experience in modern urban life is depicted: a chance conversation in a carpark in Northam, Western Australia. The poet–speaker talks with a man about tyre pressure, then how the invasive South African weed 'double-gees' (l.17) punctures bike tyres, and watches the man rescue a runaway trolley. After the stranger drives off, a woman approaches and says, *'that lot ... They're* trouble' (ll.41, 44), the first real indication that the stranger was a First Nations man. The poet–speaker defends him as 'A good bloke' (l.45), and reflects on 'this town and its / foul history' (ll.50–1). He muses, 'Brother, if you ever / read this, know I admire you' (ll.52–3).

Key point

This poem documents a casual conversation in everyday Australian speech ('bloke', l.45, and 'Gidday mate', l.5). What makes it poetry is Kinsella's philosophical rumination and his determination to identify patterns that underlie everyday experiences. He probes how small gestures contribute to the bigger picture and how individuals define the community.

Shopping Centre Carpark (Response), CPG (p.134)

Green's reply takes the same title as the previous poem, 'Shopping Centre Carpark'. It concerns the particular significance of the 'Geraldton Woollies carpark' (l.1) for Yamaji people. Pauline Hanson visited it when campaigning for conservative political party One Nation during the 2017 election. When she arrived, 'Three Yamaji women parked up in carpark / And went to do an unwelcome to country ... For Pauline Hanson One Nation Party' (ll.11–14). Referring to Kinsella's poem, Green observes, 'That party is one big Australian double-gee / As a kid I would call them jubaal-gees' (ll.18–19). The shift from to 'jubaal-gee' to 'double-gee' captures something of Green's own journey: her feet are 'A bit too soft from wearing shoes nowadays' (l.24), as she has become accustomed to comforts than many still lack.

Q How does Green's poem build on what Kinsella calls 'the politics of double gees' (Kinsella, 'Shopping Centre Carpark', p.133, l.55)?

The Wild Colonial Boy, JK (pp.135–7)

Key quote

> 'The wild colonial boy can't call Australia home, though he has never really left its shores; but he has travelled outside its jurisdictions, and he has travelled far beyond its metaphors' (ll.67–9)

This poem is paired with Green's 'A White Colonial Boy', which follows. Both reference 'The Wild Colonial Boy', a nineteenth-century Irish-Australian folk ballad about a young (white) man 'of poor but honest parents' who recognises that the colonial system keeps the working poor in 'slavery, bound down by iron chains' (Wikipedia). He becomes a bushranger but, like Robin Hood, does not rob the poor. He embodies the Australian lovable larrikin stereotype, a good bloke who is not afraid to break rules (or laws). Ultimately, he is shot by police.

Kinsella's wild colonial boy is 'a loner' who feels 'guilt over his plunder' (ll.1–2). He does not participate in the famous Eureka Stockade rebellion of 1854 (when gold prospectors in Ballarat, Victoria, defied the government, refusing to pay licence fees). Rather he is a drug-taking beneficiary of mining who 'tries to fly in and fly out but is caught out, / amphetamines in his urine' (ll.9–10). In this contemporary adaptation of the myth, the wild colonial boy finds himself in a prison cell with 'a Noongar bloke / who shares law and knowledge from country' (ll.11–12). After his release, he is arrested again, beaten up, and sees another Noongar man beaten to death. He is 'extradited as a witness / to be laughed at by the judge, to be warned to say nothing more' (ll.36–8). He 'promises himself he will shout the truth / at every footy match' (ll.40–1). Then, he 'wanders the port streets on his release, / not understanding he's in a decolonising world' (ll.43–4). He wants to 'unlearn the codes of his failings' (l.49), but struggles to separate himself from the codes of masculinity supported by a colonial system. The lines, 'a friend whose name he won't use in a song / out of respect for the dead' (ll.58–9), suggest that his friend is Aboriginal. Only silence is respectful; the words of this poem only serve white history. Recognising this, the wild colonial boy wanders 'homeless / and stateless and his family can't reach him' (ll.65–6).

The closing lines suggest that language itself is a prison. Although Kinsella expresses despair about the persistence of colonial ideology, he keeps writing.

Q How does Kinsella's poem anticipate Green's 'A White Colonial Boy'?

A White Colonial Boy, CPG (pp.138–40)

In Green's poem, the white colonial boy is also a beneficiary of the colonial system. He is a brutal, unfeeling man, who 'Arrived with the settlers / Sits at the table of invasion' (ll.2–3). He is a character type perpetually reinvented or reborn in each era. 'Multiple personalities / Drive him like a madman / Across the generations' (ll.8–10). He is a rapist. 'With steel caps stamping mob to the ground / digging deep into their back with brutal force' (ll.22–3), he enjoys 'deranged colonial delights' (l.27). He is 'wrapped in a sense of / Social media security with the likes / Comments validating his crimes' (ll.29–31), and 'perches / Like false king on his high court judge bench / Inflicting further colonial trauma' (ll.42–4). Bitterly, Green writes, 'The concept of terra nullius remains / Intact in the midst and mind of this civilised / Wild white colonial boys' club' (ll.53–5). Recalling the original 'The Wild Colonial Boy', Green asserts that the young Irish man who 'robbed the wealthy and helped the poor ... That's the real wild colonial boy' (ll.71, 73).

Q What new perspectives does Green bring to 'The Wild Colonial Boy'?

Peacocking at Ellendale Pool, JK (pp.141–2)

Kinsella's title references an interpretive sign for tourists that reads, 'A European History of Ellendale Pool: Pastoralism and Peacocking'. Ellendale Pool is a deep waterhole on the Greenough River in the Geraldton district.

The poem opens: 'Speaking a truth doesn't disabuse' (l.1), and then describes the site's natural beauty, and the tourists. The sign mentions Western Australian writer Randolph Stow (1935–2010), whose first novel *A Haunted Land* (1956) includes a scene at the Ellendale Pool. The sign informs tourists that '*desire* / troubled this enclave' and 'its bloodied history' (ll.10–11, 12). In Stow's novel, the daughter of a pastoral family has consensual sex with a First Nations man on the banks of the pool. She does not challenge her family's assumption that it is rape. Kinsella writes of Stow, 'And then he was gone, / ensconced in Suffolk' (ll.12–13), suggesting that Stow exposed ugly truths about settler–colonial race relations, but he was cowardly and left the country without doing anything about it. Of Stow's novel, Kinsella observes satirically, '"Indigenous connection" – thriller / subtext, crime drama, blockbuster and award winner' (ll.22–3). How should a white male descendant of colonial pastoralists (like Stow, or Kinsella) write of these places and histories, 'This land that never stopped being Aboriginal land, / and *it* allows us to walk its erosions' (ll.25–6)?

Q What is the meaning of the closing line, 'Such decorations of the literary! Such gifts of English!' (l.28)?

Key vocabulary

Disabuse: reveal the truth to someone who has been deceived or mistaken.

Creation Markings – Ellendale Pool, CPG (p.143)

Green's poem refers to signage and sculptures concerning Aboriginal cultural history at the Ellendale Pool. Green focuses on a sculpture of Bimara, the rainbow serpent of the Dreaming associated with waterholes and waterways, presented as a *'Significant culture marker'* (l.12). According to Green, these signs and 'Tourist furniture barbie toilet swings' (l.10) package the site as a 'hidden oasis for intruders' (l.16). She describes the site as a 'Tapestry of coexistence woven' (l.19), expressing tentative optimism about the possibility of shared stories and places. She quickly undercuts this, stressing that the Amangu history of the site has been overtaken by colonial history.

Q How do you interpret the closing line, 'Metal sculpture appeases society guilt' (l.22)?

Epilogue, JK & CPG (pp.144–5)

The epilogue (concluding segment commenting on the collection as a whole) is attributed to both authors: the reference to 'some of us who aren't traditional owners / are also torn from the inside out' (l.2–3) identifies Kinsella as the author of the first section, and the line 'This barna – our ancestors' land – our land' (l.14) in the second stanza identifies Green. Kinsella asserts, 'There can be no surrender of spiritual rights' (l.5). His ten-line stanza is followed by Green's twenty-eight-line stanza. The length of these sections reinforces Kinsella's point that Green has more right to speak to these issues.

Green accuses farmers of poisoning the land, miners of blowing it up, and highways of displacing her ancestors and history. The final line, 'Why are we still invisible?' (l.38), sums up the ethos of the whole collection.

THEMES, IDEAS & VALUES

Decolonisation

Key quotes

'... The school
was busy re-enacting Grey's
expedition but I knew
that wasn't part of my vision,
though later I'd rewrite it
as a poem of decolonisation.'
(Kinsella , 'Hawes – God's Intruder', p.39, ll.137–42)

'Young teachings perched on Walkaway hill
Space reclaiming decolonising respacing '
(Green, 'Honey to Lips Bottlebrush', p.53, ll.1–2)

'The wild colonial boy wanders the port streets on his release,
    not understanding that he's in a decolonising world,
    the shops bristling with worldly goods, with opportunities,
    and all good things coming to those standing and waiting'
(Kinsella, 'The Wild Colonial Boy', p.136, ll.43–6)

The poets directly reference the idea of decolonisation in several poems, and indirectly the concept holds the collection together. Decolonisation describes the dismantling of the great European empires that dominated the globe from the nineteenth century. Politically, this process began in the postwar period, 1945–60, when many colonies were declared independent nations. Over the following decades it became clear that the logic, ideals and ethos of empire lived on even in newly independent nations. Colonial empires may have been dismantled, but the principles upon which they were built have proven extraordinarily difficult to budge. Calls for decolonisation in the twenty-first century directly address this legacy.

Key point

The collection's title communicates the poets' attitude towards the colonial ethos that continues to define Australia. This is politically activist poetry. The poets do not incite readers to take violent action; they are on a cultural crusade aimed at raising awareness of the dark legacy of Australian colonisation.

The words 'decolonisation' and 'decolonise' signal clearly that this poetry engages directly with current postcolonial theory. This is not surprising as both writers are academically trained. They chose to communicate these ideas in poetry, however, and not in an academic paper. This gives us a clue to understanding what they think poetry can achieve.

What do Kinsella and Green mean when they talk about decolonisation? Across the globe decolonisation has been a violent process involving war, political protest and litigation, from America to India to the Soviet Union. On many occasions the poets highlight the original violence of Australia's settler–colonials. Green calls it the 'time of invasion' when 'Lands [were] stolen from traditional owners' ('Country rulers', p.9, ll.17, 13). According to Green, many Australians still try to brush this history under the carpet: 'You don't want me to talk about / Invasion of this land' ('Don't want me to talk', p.7, ll.10–11).

The foundational values accompanying the settlement of Australia as a colony of Great Britain are remarkably resilient. Sometimes they resurface even when people are consciously trying to move on. Kinsella writes:

> try not to look at the rockwork
> as an example of European art
> of the twentieth-century –
> that new colonial way
> in the claims to decolonising –
> just know that there are other ways,
> and claim no more ...

('Lake Magic Resonances (January 2017)', p.75, ll.53–9)

He asserts that decolonisation is not just a word, nor is it a simple process. It involves self-scrutiny, dialogue and mutual respect. There are many ways to approach decolonisation. Green recalls a 'decolonise[d] funeral ceremony' ('Funeral Directors', p.123, l.15), with 'a coffin in the colours ... found in Noongar country' (ll.11–12).

Decolonisation begins with dismantling the vestiges of colonial administration, then building an independent political nation, society or community in its place. As the poets emphasise, it involves constant vigilance. Kinsella gives a nuanced picture of colonial brutality, which also affected white people (for example, he describes being beaten up, in 'Hawes – God's Intruder', pp.43–5). He acknowledges that, in spite of his political sympathies, as a white man he is a beneficiary of the colonial system and therefore must let Green lead the way. For example, while he feels the grief of 'three generations / of onlookers' ('Sammies (Salmon Gums)', p.113, ll.58–9) when he watches ancient gum trees being felled, he acknowledges that First Nations peoples have a deeper and longer connection to the land and 'the Wurak' trees (p.113, l.64). Rather than buckle under the weight of this terrible history and the persistence of myths that gloss over it, Kinsella and Green offer an alternative built on respectful cross-cultural dialogue.

Yarning

Key quotes

'A campfire binds us
Swapping yarns
Silly ones to make us laugh
Serious ones about our people
Sharing ones about our cultures
We share this space'
(Green, 'Campfire', p.63, ll.1–6)

'yarning with all living things of the world
joined together: land, water, air, spirit.'
('Epilogue', p.144, ll.9–10)

Yarning is a key concept in *False Claims of Colonial Thieves*. It is mentioned in 'Hawes – God's Intruder', 'Campfire', 'Tangi', 'Simply Yarning', 'Yarn Response Poem' and 'Epilogue'. Yarning means telling stories, and it has particular significance for Noongar people who use the word to describe free-form associative conversations in which stories are exchanged. Such dialogues are defined by mutual respect. Over recent decades the concept of yarning has gained academic significance. Green's poem 'Simply Yarning' is dedicated to Dawn Bessarab, a Bard/ Yjindjabandi woman and a social worker in Aboriginal child protection. Bessarab has written academic papers advocating 'yarning' as a method in Indigenous research. Green's poem opens, 'Yarning is a beautiful conversation' ('Simply Yarning,' p.97, l.1), and closes, 'Yarning puts us on common ground / Hey come on Dawn let's have a yarn' (p.97, ll.22–3). Green credits Bessarab with providing the conceptual scaffolding that enabled her poetic conversation with Kinsella.

In 'Yarn Response Poem', Kinsella responds to Green's invitation to talk: 'How can I but take up the call, / Charmaine, and yarn right back at you –' (p.98, ll.1–2). He affirms that in yarning they share animosity towards 'the white stakeholders / in the town' (p.98, ll.5–6). He writes that his engagement with Yamaji culture extends beyond his yarning with Green to his own family. At the Yamaji Art gallery, he 'bought a couple of paintings for our son Tim, because they meant / so much to him' (p.98, ll.17–19). He continues the yarning spirit of cross-cultural communication by fostering his son's engagement with, and appreciation for, Yamaji art. He mentions another member of the yarning circle, his brother: 'You know him too, and he knows / you, and we all feel good about that' (p.99, ll.33–4). He closes respectfully, 'This is yarning too, Charmaine, / and I take my cue from you' (p.99, ll.35–6).

Key point

By yarning with Green, Kinsella marks his commitment to relinquishing white man's power by ceding linguistic control to his Yamaji collaborator.

Environmental degradation

Key quote

'Scrub, forests, / their contents. All gone. Hole.'
(Kinsella, 'Undermining', part 1, p.1, ll.9–10)

False Claims of Colonial Thieves is a collection of topographical (place-based) poems. The poems protest about the degradation of natural environments, particularly through mining, which Kinsella and Green view as colonial exploitation. They express concern about the environmental impacts, such as toxins brought to the surface, and open-cut mines.

In the co-written poem 'Undermining' (pp.1–2), Kinsella asserts that greed for uranium destroys reasonable moral principles: 'Lure of the material – to conjure empathy out of furnaces' (part 1, p.1, l.11). Mining, and the greed that drives it, is supported by a warped understanding of 'empathy' and 'religions honed as bayonets' (part 1, p.1, ll.12). In other words, mining is not geared to responsibility towards others; it blithely destroys lives. Green continues, 'Old ground our country / With ancient ones deep within' (part 2, p.2, ll.17–18), describing the First Nations peoples' understanding that the landscape is a sentient, living and feeling presence animated by the ancient spirits of elders. This image suggests that the land itself is a living repository of deep First Nations history. By disturbing the soil, open-cut mining destroys this legacy. Green asserts that 'Uranium is safe in the earth / Like a sleeping elder' (part 2, p.2, ll.38–9); the implication is that it is dangerous and destructive when unearthed.

Both Green and Kinsella object to the way that settler farms, towns and mines displaced First Nations peoples, and undermined their culture. For Green, such activities have compromised the integrity of her people. The title of her poem 'Blue Scar' (p.96) refers to how a road disfigures the flesh of the land; she sees a 'Bitumen urban mess on country' (l.2). Roads represent the 'cultural mindset' (l.3) of the

'Whiteman's presence' (l.7) on traditional land. Drugs and crime take hold of urban First Nations individuals because their connection to their land and culture has been weakened – see, for example, 'Needle Teacher' (p.118) and 'Dark Light Bulbs' (pp.119–20).

In 'Sammies' (pp.111–13) Kinsella describes how the felling of ancient trees triggers the grief of 'three generations / of onlookers' (ll.58–9) but acknowledges the deeper knowledge and connection of First Nations peoples. Deforestation is another form of environmental degradation with deep social effects.

Defining poetry through allusion and intertextuality

Key quote

'wagtails over the Rubicon,
"the die is cast",
gold and mines so deep
they drowned.'
(Kinsella, 'Niagara Dam Poems', p.15, ll.10–13)

In *False Claims of Colonial Thieves* Green and Kinsella make many allusions to other works of literature, art and popular culture. This is a technique used by many artists and creators to define their own creative practice and outputs, by positioning them in relation to what has come before.

Sometimes the intertextual references are a way of paying a debt or acknowledging a formative influence. This is the case with Kinsella's reference to Frank O'Hara (1926–66), a twentieth-century American poet and art curator, and a leading figure in the New York School – an avant-garde cultural movement. Kinsella writes, 'Frank O'Hara made street corners / of topography' ('The Artlessness of Internal Travel', p.80, ll.79–80); in other words, O'Hara's poetic oeuvre (body of work) provides a model for autobiographical topographical poetry in which the self is realised (gains definition) through its connection to places.

Kinsella transmutes O'Hara's urban topography (New York street corners) into his own non-urban location: the outback topography of the Mullewa–Geraldton district. By dedicating 'Simply Yarning' (p.97) to Dawn Bessarab, Green similarly acknowledges intertextual references, making it clear that she blends threads from Bessarab's writing into her poem.

At other points the intertextual allusions are more subtle. Kinsella alludes to classical literature in his 'Niagara Dam Poems'. Looking at the 'rare water on the edge / of the desert' (p.15, ll.4–5) in the Eastern Goldfields of Western Australia, he imagines he sees another famous river: the Rubicon. These lines establish the idea that the creation of the Niagara Dam in the desert riverbed set an irreversible course of events in train. In Roman history, the crossing of the Rubicon (a river in northern Italy) was a point at which Julius Caesar stood at the brink of irreversible change, and paused to consider the consequences of his action. In crossing the river against the orders of Rome, Caesar set the Roman Civil War in motion, and assumed dictatorial powers. So, the crossing of the Rubicon was the last moment before the destruction of war was unleashed and a totalitarian regime imposed upon Rome. Here in Kinsella's poem, the rare desert 'wagtails' (small native Australian birds) cross the dry riverbed, and Kinsella cites the words attributed to Caesar, 'the die is cast', meaning fate is sealed. The dam supports the mining industry: it was built to supply water for the steam engines needed to transport 'gold [from] mines so deep' (l.12). The Rubicon, as alluded to in this context, symbolises a line between innocence and experience, peace and war, natural landscape and its destruction for economic gain. In this example, intertextuality gives weight to the poem's message.

In contrast, Green makes a number of pop culture references – to songs and folk stories, for example. Her poem 'Fluoro girl world' (p.13) opens: 'I am not a fluoro girl / Living in a fluoro world' (ll.1–2), alluding to both the chorus of Madonna's 1985 hit 'Material girl' – 'Cause we are living in a material world / And I am a material girl' – as well as the chorus of Aqua's 1997 song 'Barbie Girl' – 'I'm a Barbie girl / In a Barbie world'. At first, this reference to pop music seems light and trivial, but in Green's poem 'material' and 'Barbie' are replaced with 'fluoro', and 'I am' is negated: this is *not* a fluoro girl. This signals a more serious message. The poet sees the fluoro colours of the mandatory safety gear worn at mine sites as a sinister echo of the fluorescent fashions of the 1980s and 90s. This fluoro gear is worn 'Driving a big truck / Making big mining bucks' (ll.3–4). Green cites familiar pop songs celebrating the embrace of capitalist consumerism in order to link it to mining (as another manifestation of capitalism), and to reject both. Here Green defines her poetry against the texts she references.

Another form of intertextuality, ekphrasis, is used in the poetic description of a work of art. Both poets write about Julie Dowling's painting in positive terms (Green, 'Old Girl', p.94; and Kinsella, 'On Julie Dowling's *My White Friend*, Geraldton Regional Gallery, 2017', p.105). In contrast, Kinsella describes his 'Reconstruction of the *Foundation of Perth 1829*, Painted by George Pitt Morison for the Centenary of 1929' as 'a poem against ekphrasis' (p.85) and dedicates it to Kim Scott. Through these multilayered intertextual allusions he rejects the values upheld by the 1929 painting, and aligns his poem with the values expressed by Noongar novelist Kim Scott.

DIFFERENT INTERPRETATIONS

Different interpretations arise from different responses to a text. Over time, a text will evoke a wide range of responses from its readers, who may come from various social or cultural groups and live in very different places and historical periods. Responses by critics and reviewers can be published in newspapers, journals and books, both online and in print. They can also be expressed in discussions among readers in the media, classrooms, book groups and so on.

While there is no single correct reading or interpretation of a text, it is important to understand that an interpretation is more than a personal opinion – it is the justification of a point of view on the text. To present an interpretation of a text based on your point of view, you must use a logical argument and support it with relevant evidence from the text.

The critics' viewpoints

False Claims of Colonial Thieves has received several positive newspaper and journal reviews. Literary critic Dan Disney described the collection as a 'fervently necessary political intervention' in current discussions of Australian identity and history (Disney 2018). First Nations writer and critic Jeanine Leane hailed it as a 'long overdue conversation Australia needs to have between the Country's First Peoples and the settler-invaders' (Leane 2020, p.1) to reconcile 'layers of pain, grief and revenge to work towards a shared history' (p.3), using poetry to probe deeper 'as history cannot' (p.4). Wiradjuri writer Brenda Saunders judged it 'a consistently strong collection' in which 'two Australian poets from different cultures ... tackle the subject of colonisation head on' (Saunders 2018, p.190); she asserts that in doing so, the poets 'illuminate the darkest places of our collective history' (p.192). Poet Laurie Keim commended the fact that, although Kinsella and Green's conceptions of 'country and land are separated by a schism of cultural practice and accumulated history ... the beauty of the book is the courage to push on through pain and loss and see if an understanding is possible'.

Two interpretations

Interpretation 1: *False Claims of Colonial Thieves* suggests that the legacy of colonialism is insurmountable.

At times the tone of *False Claims of Colonial Thieves* is profoundly negative. Green emphasises this in the repeated refrain, 'Arrived as colonial thieves / Remain as colonial thieves' ('Always thieves', p.127, ll.7–8). According to Kinsella, evil is inherent in the government: 'The state is killing our souls / The state has murdered the people – some they murder over and / over' ('A New Ode to Westralia: Anthem for All Future Sporting Events', p.125, ll.1–3). Both poets agree that colonial settlement was a brutal, violent and deeply unjust appropriation of First Nations lands; the occupants were 'displaced and alienated / From traditional country' (Green, 'Hawes – God's Intruder', p.42, ll.223–4).

The poets view Christianity as part of the colonial machine. This is communicated in the poems about the churches in the Mullewa–Geraldton district. As Kinsella writes, 'prayers shake down the land into farms and a cradle / of wheat' ('Bottlebrush Behind Our Lady of Fatima Church, Nanson, Chapman Valley', p.51, ll.12–13), suggesting that religion attempted to legitimise settler–colonial claims to First Nations lands.

Both poets see the colonial legacy living on in contemporary society. Of the mining industry, Green writes, 'Don't mind me Australia / I just don't care for mining / And your colonial bulldust' ('Don't mine me', p.14, ll.1–3). She also documents how suffering was created for contemporary First Nations peoples with the introduction of drugs ('Drug Slaves' p.117, and 'Needle Teacher', p.118); some argue over degrees of belonging ('Identity Police', p.116), and others work for white corporations for short-term gain ('Monitoring Lizards', p.124). The descendants of white settlers, such as Kinsella, are uncertain about what actions, if any, they can take to undercut persistent colonial values. This is evident in his environmental activism; he writes *'the ancient salmon gums are killed off – death-wish / where roads are widened to "prevent deaths"?'* (epigraph to 'Sammies (Salmon Gums)', p.111). These poems express powerlessness in the face of systemic destruction and damage.

Interpretation 2: *False Claims of Colonial Thieves* suggests that there is hope for the future.

Although *False Claims of Colonial Thieves* can seem relentlessly negative as it describes how the brutal and racist legacy of colonialism continues to determine attitudes, cultural practice and the distribution of wealth in contemporary Australian society, the poets express hope for a better future. Green's directive, 'It's a shared true history – let's heal' ('Don't want me to talk', p.7, ll.12) is addressed to her collaborator, Kinsella, but also to her readers.

Kinsella stresses that this healing must involve rewriting the stories about Australian settlement. He asserts: 'Those of us with colonisers / as ancestors look for ways to retell / their stories, to build hope' ('Grandmothers', p.5, ll.58–60). To this end he wrestles with local and familial stories as well as big-picture narratives of the birth of modern Australia. As Green explains, the way forward is to 'stitch a new robe / To wear and heal together / On this land we both call home' ('Third Space', p.101, ll.44–6); that is, to bring different voices, experiences and stories together. This poetry collection models collaborative, cross-cultural storytelling as a way forward.

QUESTIONS & ANSWERS

This section focuses on your own analytical writing on the text, and gives you strategies for producing high-quality responses in your coursework and exam essays.

Essay writing – an overview

An essay on a literary work is a formal and serious piece of writing that presents your point of view on the text, usually in response to a given topic. Your 'point of view' in an essay is your interpretation of the meaning of the text's language, structure, characters, situations and events, supported by detailed analysis of textual evidence.

Analyse – don't summarise

In your essays it is important to avoid simply summarising what happens in a text.

- A **summary** is a description or paraphrase (retelling in different words) of the characters and events. For example: 'Macbeth has a horrifying vision of a dagger dripping with blood before he goes to murder King Duncan.'
- An **analysis** is an explanation of the real meaning or significance that lies 'beneath' the text's words (and images, for a film). For example: 'Macbeth's vision of a bloody dagger shows how deeply uneasy he is about the violent act he is contemplating, and conveys his sense that supernatural forces are impelling him to act.'

A limited amount of summary is sometimes necessary to let your reader know which part of the text you wish to discuss. However, always keep this to a minimum and follow it immediately with your analysis of what this part of the text is really telling us.

Plan your essay

Carefully plan your essay so that you have a clear idea of what you are going to say. The plan ensures that your ideas flow logically, that your argument remains consistent and that you stay on the topic. An essay plan should be a list of **brief dot points** covering no more than half a page.

- Include your central argument or main contention – a concise statement of your overall response to the topic.
- Write three or four dot points for each paragraph, indicating the main idea and evidence/examples from the text. Note that in your essay you will need to *expand* on these points and *analyse* the evidence.

Structure your essay

An essay is a complete, self-contained piece of writing. It has a clear beginning (the introduction), middle (several body paragraphs) and end (the last paragraph or conclusion). It must also have a central argument that runs throughout, linking each paragraph to form a coherent whole. See examples of introductions and conclusions in the 'Analysing a sample topic' and 'Sample answer' sections.

The introduction establishes your overall response to the topic. It includes your main contention and outlines the main evidence you will refer to in the course of the essay. Write your introduction *after* you have done a plan and *before* you write the rest of the essay.

The body paragraphs argue your case – they present evidence from the text and explain how this evidence supports your argument. Each body paragraph needs:

- a strong **topic sentence** (usually the first sentence) that states the main point being made in the paragraph
- **evidence** from the text, including some brief quotations
- **analysis** of the textual evidence, with **explanation** of its significance and how it supports your argument
- **links back to the topic** in one or more statements, usually towards the end of the paragraph.

Connect the body paragraphs so that your discussion flows smoothly. Use some linking words and phrases such as 'similarly' and 'on the other hand', though don't start every paragraph like this. Another strategy is to use a significant word from the last sentence of one paragraph in the first sentence of the next.

Use key terms from the topic – or synonyms for them – throughout, so the relevance of your discussion to the topic is always clear.

The conclusion ties everything together and finishes the essay. It includes strong statements that emphasise your central argument and provide a clear response to the topic.

Avoid simply restating the points made earlier in the essay – this will end on a very flat note and imply that you have run out of ideas and vocabulary. The conclusion should be a logical extension of what you have written, not just a repetition or summary of it. Writing an effective conclusion can be a challenge. Try using these tips:

- Start by linking back to the final sentence of the second-last paragraph – this helps your writing to flow, rather than leaping back to your main contention straight away.
- Use synonyms and expressions with equivalent meanings to vary your vocabulary. This allows you to reinforce your line of argument without being repetitive.
- When planning your essay, think of one or two broad statements or observations about the text's wider meaning. These should be related to the topic and your overall argument. Keep them for the conclusion, since they will give you something 'new' to say but still follow logically from your discussion. The introduction will be focused on the topic, but the conclusion can present a wider view of the text.

Essay topics

1. 'In *False Claims of Colonial Thieves* Charmaine Papertalk Green and John Kinsella rewrite European and First Nations Australian myths in order to unsettle colonial values.' Discuss.
2. In what sense is Green and Kinsella's co-written poem 'Hawes – God's Intruder' "a poem of decolonisation"?
3. "Yarning puts us on common ground". How does the concept of yarning hold the collection together?
4. *False Claims of Colonial Thieves* is unified in its aims, yet the poets' voices remain distinct. Discuss.
5. 'The role of poetry is to give pleasure.' How well does this statement sum up Charmaine Papertalk Green and John Kinsella's *False Claims of Colonial Thieves*?
6. 'Good poetry ... speaks to the emotions as well as to the intellect. It can also pierce the armour of resistance to the way things are usually perceived'.
   How accurate is this account of *False Claims of Colonial Thieves*?
7. According to Charmaine Papertalk Green and John Kinsella, what are the false claims of colonial thieves?
8. What is the significance of place in *False Claims of Colonial Thieves*?
9. 'In *False Claims of Colonial Thieves* personal identity derives from country.' Discuss.
10. '*False Claims of Colonial Thieves* exposes fault lines at the heart of Australian colonialism.' Discuss.

Vocabulary for writing on *False Claims of Colonial Thieves*

First Nations peoples: an appropriate term to refer to the ethnicity of the original Australians. The text uses the term Aboriginal so this is also acceptable in direct quotations or other close references to the text.

Another term that has become acceptable in the recent past (so may be used by critics and other commentators) is Aboriginal and Torres Strait Islander peoples. It is not considered appropriate to use the term Aborigine due its connotations within Australia's colonial history.

Decolonisation: the dismantling of the great European empires that dominated the globe from the nineteenth century.

Intertextuality: references to other texts; this adds layers of meaning.

Settler–colonial: member of a group of new settlers who displace original inhabitants of a place.

Yarning: telling stories; an important practice for many First Nations peoples.

Analysing a sample topic

"Yarning puts us on common ground". How does the concept of yarning hold the collection together?

To answer this question you will need to provide a definition of the concept of yarning, and discuss the degree to which it connects the poems in the collection. You need to consider what Green and Kinsella say about yarning and how they demonstrate the practice in their writing.

Sample introduction

> When First Nations Australians meet one another, it is traditional to swap stories to explain their histories and define themselves. This is yarning as defined by Charmaine Papertalk Green and academic Dawn Bessarab. The key concept is that all participants within a yarning conversation are, as Green explains, 'on common ground'. All participants tell their stories and are given respect. In *False Claims of Colonial Thieves,* Green (a Yamaji woman) and John Kinsella (a descendant of white settlers) exchange stories through their poems. Their hope is that poetry built upon respectful

dialogue can chart a way forward, redefine Australian culture, and destabilise the colonial values that persist in contemporary life. In this collection yarning builds common ground through language, dialogue, the reframing of histories and the telling of stories that respect difference.

Body paragraph outline

Paragraph 1: Language

Discuss textual examples that illustrate how the poems manifest the principle of yarning, or shared storytelling, in their respectful intercultural dialogue. Consider 'Simply Yarning' and 'Yarn Response Poem' in detail. Explain how yarning is represented through dialogue, familiar language, and the mixing of Yamaji and English.

Paragraph 2: Poetic dialogue

Explain how the dialogue between the poets exemplifies the concept of yarning as 'common ground': relevant quotes include 'Yarning is a beautiful conversation' (Green, 'Simply Yarning', p.97, l.1) and 'This is yarning, too, Charmaine' (Kinsella, 'Yarn Response Poem', p.99, l.35). Explain how the notion of 'different but equal' shapes the dialogue, for example, in mixing First Nations language with English, and also in mixing Yamaji and white settler histories and culture.

Paragraph 3: Yarning and history

Explain how yarning offers an alternative possibility in terms of negotiating colonial attitudes to race relations. Both poets protest the past treatment of First Nations peoples and their cultures and histories: 'Past injustices, cultural cruelty, cultural genocide / And the cultural pain that is left behind' (Green, 'Don't want me to talk', p.7, ll.14–15). Kinsella describes how Australia's 'bloodied history' implicates descendants of white settlers, like himself ('Peacocking at Ellendale Pool', p.141, l.12).

Paragraph 4: Shared stories

Argue that yarning is a forward-looking, optimistic way to develop stories that will support a more egalitarian multicultural society in which different cultures and histories are respected. Textual evidence could include:

- 'Finding time to walk over / Each other's barna' (Green, 'I won't pretend', p.62, ll.16–17) – that is, respectfully acknowledging each culture's traditions, places and histories
- 'Poetry as an artform / Was intended to make up / For what was lost in the taking' (Kinsella, 'Histories', p.31, ll.85–7) – according to Kinsella, poetry can redress the colonial violation that shaped Australian history and culture
- 'This reaches out to you, Ms Dhu, / and to all those from past and present / who hold you close, who won't / see you lost in the files' (Kinsella, 'In Marapikurrinya: for Ms Dhu', p.130, ll.37–40).

Sample conclusion

In *False Claims of Colonial Thieves*, Green and Kinsella develop a dialogue across a collection of poems. Both poets speak for themselves and tell their own history. This is 'yarning': the mutually respectful exchange of stories that define one's culture, history and heritage. Common ground is established through respect and thoughtful responses, with the poets offering their dialogue as a model for an ideal society in which difference is respected. Significantly, this conversation takes place on 'common ground' and many of the poems make it clear that the ground, or the earth itself, is hosting the dialogue; as Kinsella writes, 'This land ... never stopped being Aboriginal land, / and *it* allows us to walk its erosions' ('Peacocking at Ellendale Pool'). Green and Kinsella propose that, by respecting one another and the natural environment, the false claims of colonial thieves may be dismantled once and for all.

SAMPLE ANSWER

What is the significance of place in *False Claims of Colonial Thieves*?

Place is crucial to the poems that make up Charmaine Papertalk Green and John Kinsella's collection, *False Claims of Colonial Thieves*. Most poems refer to at least one particular place; many specifically mention the Mullewa–Geraldton region in Western Australia to which both poets have strong familial links. The poems do not simply describe physical locations, however. They also probe the significance of each place to each poet, and to Australian culture generally. Some places are significant in the Dreaming or First Nations histories, some to settler–colonial history, and others resonate for both cultures. Examining intersections of significance involves consideration of the politics of fraught histories of land, churches, buildings and waterways, and evaluation of what those places represent. Some of those mentioned have complex and multilayered histories reaching back through First Nations Dreaming to white settlement in Australia and up to the present.

False Claims of Colonial Thieves is a collection of topographical poetry: poetry concerned with describing places and probing the deeper cultural meanings of those places. The poems consider how certain areas in the Mullewa–Geraldton district shape the identity of the region and the people associated with it. Whereas Green considers this from the perspective of Yamaji people, Kinsella interrogates the white settler–colonial attitudes instilled in him. Both poets view place as a complex and politically fraught issue. Rather than celebrate places for their intrinsic beauty, the poets ask readers to be aware of the submerged values and histories associated with those places.

Places that represent First Nations peoples' histories and beliefs carry a particular significance in this collection, highlighting the prior claim of First Nations peoples to land later claimed by white settlers under the legal justification of terra nullius – the idea that the land was uninhabited and that First Nations peoples did not have a concept of land ownership. This justification is contested in the collection. For example, Green explains that the location of Mass Rock, the place where Monsignor Hawes held open-air services for First Nations converts to Roman Catholicism, has a longer prior history for Yamaji people. She writes 'Mass Rock is the intruder in our space / Mass Rock is not my significant site / My people's campsite not Hawes' space' ('No other road'). This place was a campsite and a meeting grounds long before white settlers arrived in the district. Signage erected at Ellendale Pool gestures at the significance of the site for Amangu people. The signs are geared towards tourists but Green observes that 'Open eyes see land talking back' ('Creation Markings – Ellendale Pool'). Careful observers can see a 'Mythical track moving across land', although Green notes that the 'Colonised story' is given prominence at the site.

The settler–colonial places described in these poems include farms, mines, churches, towns and roads. Green describes a road as a 'Blue Scar' marking the landscape with the 'cultural mindset' of the 'Whiteman's presence' on traditional land ('Blue Scar'). For Kinsella, too, colonisation leaves a mixed legacy. His family farmed in the Mullewa region, then worked in the mines. He is ambivalent about these industries, due to the environmental damage they wreak. As a person 'with colonisers / as ancestors' ('Grandmothers'), he would like 'to build hope', but he cannot view the impacts of colonialism and capitalism with nostalgia. He is painfully aware that the original inhabitants were displaced from country through white settlement, and that neither farming nor mining benefits First Nations peoples as a whole. For this reason, both poets see such activities as part of a colonial, capitalist mindset that exploits the land and people for profit, and is supported by Christianity. Contrary to the Church's stated commitment to care, Kinsella sees a church in Mullewa as a sinister 'colonial theatre / of cruelty' ('Our Lady of Mt Carmel, Mullewa'). While farms, mines, churches, towns and roads are products and symbols of colonialism, they can also have historical significance – albeit often negative – for First Nations peoples.

The collection describes several places from the contrasting perspectives of Green and Kinsella. This is the case in the discussion of the churches associated with Monsignor Hawes in Mullewa and Geraldton but also for more contemporary spaces, as, for example, in 'Shopping Centre Carpark' and its response. In the first 'Shopping Centre Carpark' poem, Kinsella describes a chance meeting with a man (presumably a First Nations man, although this is not stated directly) and observes as the man rescues a runaway shopping trolley, preventing an accident. This simple thoughtful act makes Kinsella consider how small gestures contribute to the bigger picture and how individual actions define the community. In 'Shopping Centre Carpark (Response)', Green focuses on the particular significance of the 'Geraldton Woollies' carpark for Yamaji people; it is a meeting place for a 'Big mob'. When One Nation politician Pauline Hanson visited during her 2017 election campaign, 'Three Yamaji women' performed 'an unwelcome to country'. Here, at an ordinary unremarkable carpark, a small-scale local protest challenging political values caught public attention and shifted public perceptions. Both these poems about shopping centre carparks highlight how such everyday places and acts define contemporary Australia.

Place is a key theme in *False Claims of Colonial Thieves*. The poems describe a range of places with significance for Yamaji people and for descendants of white settlers, as well as places that have significance for both groups. Throughout, Green and Kinsella present places as First Nations land – 'barna' in Yamaji language – that is unceded; the collection exposes terra nullius as one of the key false claims of colonial thieves.

REFERENCES & READING

The text

Green, CP & Kinsella, J 2018, *False Claims of Colonial Thieves,* Magabala Books, Broome, Western Australia.

References & further reading

Anon 1899, 'Ode to Westralia', first published in the Kalgoorlie Sun, https://www.warrenfahey.com.au/land-of-forests-fleas-and-flies/

Anon (n.d.), 'The Wild Colonial Boy', https://en.wikipedia.org/wiki/The_Wild_Colonial_Boy

Bessarab, D & Ng'andu, B 2010, 'Yarning about Yarning as a Legitimate Method in Indigenous Research', *International Journal of Critical Indigenous Studies*, vol. 3, no. 1, pp.37–50.

Disney, D 2018, 'Charmaine Papertalk Green and John Kinsella: *False Claims of Colonial Thieves*', *World Literature Today*, vol. 92, no.5, pp.87–8.

Eagleton, T 2002, *Marxism and Literary Criticism*, Routledge, London. First published 1976.

Horne, D 1976, *The Death of the Lucky Country*, Penguin, Sydney.

Keim, L 2018, 'Review: *False Claims of Colonial Thieves*', *Independent Australian*, 10 March, https://independentaustralia.net/life/art-display/review-false-claims-of-colonial-thieves

Leane, J 2020, '*False Claims of Colonial Thieves* by Charmaine Papertalk Green and John Kinsella (2018)', *Swamphen*, vol. 7, pp.1–4.

Murray, L 1982, *The Vernacular Republic: Poems* 1961–1981, Angus & Robertson, Sydney.

Nichols, C 2018, 'Conversation and colonisation: poets Charmaine Papertalk Green and John Kinsella', 24 July, https://www.abc.net.au/radionational/programs/the-book-show/false-claims-of-colonial-thieves/9869410

O'Dowd, MF & Heckenberg, R 2020, 'Explainer: what is decolonisation?' *The Conversation*, 23 June, https://theconversation.com/explainer-what-is-decolonisation-131455

Saunders, B 2018, 'Review of *False Claims of Colonial Thieves*', *Westerly*, vol. 63 no. 1, pp.190–4.